# THE
# ASHES
# FILES

# THE
# ASHES
# FILES

## STEVEN FINN

### WITH MATT ROLLER

SEVEN DIALS

First published in Great Britain in 2025 by Seven Dials,
an imprint of The Orion Publishing Group Ltd
Carmelite House, 50 Victoria Embankment
London EC4Y 0DZ

An Hachette UK Company

The authorised representative in the EEA is Hachette Ireland,
8 Castlecourt Centre, Dublin 15, D15 XTP3,
Ireland (email: info@hbgi.ie)

1  3  5  7  9  10  8  6  4  2

A CIP catalogue record for this book is
available from the British Library.

Written by Matt Roller

ISBN (Hardback) 978 1 3996 3779 4
ISBN (Export Trade Paperback) 978 1 3996 3796 1
ISBN (Ebook) 978 1 3996 3781 7
ISBN (Audio) 978 1 3996 3782 4

Typeset at The Spartan Press Ltd,
Lymington, Hants

Printed and bound in Great Britain by Clays Ltd,
Elcograf S.p.A.

www.orionbooks.co.uk

*To Amber and Kora*

# Contents

# Prologue

**18 January 2014. Departures, Brisbane Airport.**

I had landed in Australia in late October, and I was finally about to fly home. I was twenty-four years old, four years into my career as an international cricketer, and had arrived full of hope that I could help England win a fourth consecutive Ashes series. We lost 5–0. I didn't play a single Test match. My England one-day coach, Ashley Giles, told me at the start of this week that I was going home ahead of schedule, then told the press that I was 'not selectable' in my current state. He was right, of course, even if I'd rather he hadn't said it publicly. I was a shell of a man: physically, mentally and emotionally drained after everything that I had put myself through.

This wasn't the end for me. I am fucking proud of the fact that it wasn't. Eighteen months later, I was back at my best: I was named man of the match after taking six second-innings wickets in our win over Australia at Edgbaston, and then celebrated on the podium at The Oval after being part of an Ashes series win for the third time. Not many England players can say that. And not many of those that can went through what I did to reach that point. After the rut I fell into, it took all my resilience to fight my way out of it and make my way back again.

1

# PROLOGUE

But I still carry the scars of that 2013/14 trip to Australia all these years later. It still hurts to look back at the hollowed-out version of myself that I became on that trip; to remember the paranoia of the young man who felt like he had the eyes of the world trained on him every time he left his hotel room; and to think how the simple act of bowling a cricket ball, the skill I had loved and was so desperate to perfect, turned into something complicated that was no longer in my control.

I kept diaries throughout my first two Ashes tours, and I'll use them in this book to help tell you my story. They are a brutally honest insight into how I was feeling, and how playing international cricket changed me – both for better and for worse.

So it only feels right that I should start by peeling my outer shell back and showing you the letter that I wrote to myself before that flight home from Brisbane. This was the final entry of my diary from the 2013/14 Ashes tour, the lowest point I reached before the battle to rebuild my career – and my life – really began. It will help you understand the extent of the mess that I had got myself into, and show you what playing international sport can do to someone. The pressure and expectation never go away, but they reach a new level during an Ashes series – even more so on the other side of the world.

When I finished writing, I put a sleeping pill on my tongue, and took a selfie for posterity. I felt the pill's numbing effect take hold of my body, allowing me to forget the world outside and the state I had got myself into. This book is the story of how I went from being one of the most promising young fast bowlers in the world to rock bottom – and then made my way right back to the top.

# PROLOGUE

**Jan 2014. Final thought – where do I go now?**

As I sit here in the departures lounge of Brisbane Airport, I can afford myself the luxury of looking back on a three-month period that started with great hope, and finished being the most depressing, demoralising three months of my life. Slowly sucking the life out of me to the point of breaking down in tears every time someone asked me about bowling, or cricket in general.

How did I get to be in this place? The tour started with great hope. Hope that I could regain my place in the Test team and be part of something very special for English cricket.

Looking back at it, I put myself under too much pressure from ball one. It is very easy for me to sit here and say this now, but I feel that I have slowly filtered out anything that was natural about my bowling action; from my slightly angled run-up, to my use of my long levers, or my athletic running to the crease and the snap that gets me my zip at the crease. I really wish I had noticed this earlier, and I hate myself for it, but I persisted.

Yes, I have had to address certain issues with my bowling. But I have always overcome these things on my own terms and in my own way.

We cannot blame me kicking the stumps for this – not solely. The real root of the problem lies further down the line, in my eyes; I wasn't happy with it, but I was backed into a corner. I felt like I had no choice. I will regret this day for the rest of my life, because it is where it started.

It was the practice day before an ODI against New Zealand in Napier, in February 2013. We were on the practice wickets, across the road from the stadium, and I was bowling in the nets. To this point, I had always had a jump into the crease. I was probably four or five mph down on where I

3

was pre-Christmas in India, when I had a back issue. I was searching for answers as to why I had lost a little bit of pace. Stupidly, I wasn't satisfied with what I had. I wanted more. That day, I tried a short run-up. Sakes* had been in my ear for a little while about shortening my run-up; he said I was doing unnecessary miles, when I could bowl the same pace off a short run-up. It made sense, but I didn't go about it the right way.

Rather than approaching the crease in a controlled, relaxed manner, as I always had done, I sprinted to the crease. The idea was to gain momentum. This would stop the jump in and it would help me maintain my pace for a longer period of time. Great, problem solved.

The best thing that could have happened to me here would have been that I'd bowled a big pile of shit, so I could just forget the short run-up and go back to doing what I'd always done. I am convinced that, if that had happened, then I wouldn't be sitting here now writing this. I would be sitting in the hotel in Sydney debriefing yesterday's game. I wouldn't have the feelings of shame and guilt that I am now experiencing. And it hurts, it hurts like fuck that I have got myself into this mess.

So, what damage did the short run-up do?

It made me do something that I have never done in my life when I bowl – force it. I was busting a gut to bowl fast. After all, it was what I was in the team for. But I have always relied on what God gave me to bowl fast. From the age of seventeen through to twenty-one, I came back every season faster. Not because I was trying to bowl fast, but because it was naturally

---

\* David Saker, England bowling coach.

happening. Now I was trying to speed up my development by doing something artificial.

I bowled nicely that day, and I stuck with it. But the warning signs were there: I started grooving bad habits, and my delivery stride became short. At the time, I thought the short run-up was helping me be strong at the crease. It wasn't. It was making me do something unnatural. I had always flowed through the crease. Now, I was jerky. Basically, I made everything short. I lost everything I had in my advantage.

I persisted with this for the remainder of the tour and into the summer. When I came back to England, I didn't feel right. I bowled a ball against Derbyshire at Lord's from the Pavilion End. It barely hit the cut strip. I smelt a rotten egg but couldn't work out what was wrong. It only happened once that day, but I lost my nip, my trust in what I was doing. Then, the same thing happened against Surrey at Lord's. Halfway through that game, Gus* and Jono** took me on to the balcony and said that the short run-up didn't suit me and that something didn't look right. I agreed, I could feel it.

The problem was that the damage had been done. I came off my long run and everything was a little bit longer, but not where it should have been. I came off the field during a fielding innings at Edgbaston, sat in the dark shower room, and cried.

I suppose this is the first time I felt myself in a really dark place. I didn't know what to do. I was a week from the first Test of the biggest summer of my life and I was bowling as badly as I'd ever bowled. But I stuck with it.

---

\* Angus Fraser, Middlesex's director of cricket.
\*\* Richard Johnson, Middlesex's bowling coach.

# PROLOGUE

I have always worked my bowling issues out by myself. I still kept faith that I could bowl myself through it. The place I am in now is a result of me having this attitude for the last nine months. I am shattered and drained from doing this every waking hour for this long.

I persisted on the same path until I was dropped from the second Test of the Ashes in the UK. I had to find a solution. I cannot have become a shit bowler in the space of five or six months.

I went to a cricket club in Bristol to meet with Jono and Shiney.* We worked on my run-up, and solely my run-up. I felt better come the end of the session. I had some dark and frustrating times during the next few weeks. But we made the run-up nice. That is now ingrained in me. My run-up is fluent, nice pace, good-length strides. A solid base to work from.

I went back to county cricket and bowled better. I had confidence in what I was doing again. I bowled quickly and skilfully. I felt I had a bit of my old zip back. I could make people hop around. In retrospect, this period glossed over the real problem.

But it shows I'm a fighter. If I'm honest, I haven't bowled like I want to bowl, or how I can bowl, since I changed to the short run-up at Napier in New Zealand. But I've fought through it. I have still bowled spells and balls that can get the best players in the world out, all while I've been confused about the problem.

It is only now that I sit on the plane that I can look back and be clear about what has got me into this situation. I am fully to blame for this. I am not shifting responsibility.

---

* Kevin Shine, ECB fast-bowling lead.

# PROLOGUE

I have always coached myself to a certain extent. Allowing myself to turn to a short run-up was the first time I had let someone from the outside influence my bowling. But it was my decision not to filter that information. That is something I won't let happen again: I appreciate people's help and goodwill, but this is my career.

The thought of people sitting around a table talking about what is best for my future now makes me angry.

On this tour I have turned to lots of people for advice. I have listened to more people than I have listened to before. I have tried every suggestion: coming slightly wider of the crease; angling my run-up slightly; lengthening my delivery stride; changing the path of my bowling arm; saying, 'Just fuck it'; sprinting to the crease; even singing while I bowl, and one hundred other things. I have never, ever been thinking of so many things when I've run up and bowled before; I've had a clear head, because I've trusted what I do. I have been searching for that golden bullet, but it doesn't exist.

I need to go back to the start. I need to make what I used to do feel natural again. The only way I am going to do this is by hours of work – but the right work. And that is for me to sit down and work it out. If I can get that ingrained back into my system, if I can get back to a place where it looks and feels natural and flowing again, I can be a better bowler than before.

But it HAS to be ingrained into my system, and I can't ever forget that feeling because it is the key to what I can achieve and how far I can go.

Basically, this is a technical problem. I do not have an issue with trust or confidence. You get both of those things from bowling well, from bowling as well as you know you can bowl and how you want to bowl. And, to be quite frank, I haven't been doing that for around twelve months.

People have written me off at the moment. People are looking at me wondering if I can ever be a good bowler again. Write me off at your peril. I will come back from this.

As you'll discover, I still wasn't admitting the full extent of my problems to anyone – even myself. But I was right: I did come back from it, not that it came easy. I spent hours and hours that spring stripping things back and re-learning how to bowl fast, but I was back in an England shirt again sooner than I could ever have hoped. Those hard yards made the highs taste even sweeter, and no feeling will ever compare to the one I experienced on my return to the Ashes in 2015. If I could re-live one week from my career, it would be that Test match at Edgbaston: the euphoria of taking a wicket in my first over back, the noise of the crowd sweeping me to the crease as I bounded in and the sense of sticking all of that criticism back down people's throats.

It is only when you sit back and reflect on a sporting career that you realise just how much pressure you are under at such a young age: I made my Middlesex debut at sixteen, my England debut at twenty and I played my last international match a month after turning twenty-eight. It tells you how heavy the burden of expectations weighed on me that I can look back and feel unfulfilled after playing for my country more than 120 times, and after taking over 250 international wickets. It is still a hard thing to get my head around. Maybe that was just how it was meant to be for me.

But I am not looking for any sympathy, and I have never, ever blamed anyone apart from myself for any of the lows that I went through. The feelings that you experience at the top level of international sport take time to process, and I understand a lot of those emotions better with distance from them. This isn't a sob story. These are just my honest, vulnerable reflections on a career that I can look back on now with a hell of a lot of pride.

# 1

# Called Up

I was lounging around in bed when the call that was about to change my life popped up on my phone. 'I'm not picking that up,' I said to myself. 'No chance.' I had a few days off between an England Lions tour to Dubai and Middlesex's boot camp on Dartmoor, pre-season training ahead of the 2010 summer. Aged twenty, I didn't have much interest in picking up the phone to a number I didn't recognise – I never did that. The same number rang again soon after, and I ignored it again.

Then my landline went. Suddenly I was in a panic. I was in my first flat, a little two-bed in Abbots Langley, Hertfordshire, and the only people who knew that number were my parents. Had something happened to one of them? I rushed to the phone. It was my mum. 'What are you doing?' she said. 'Geoff Miller's just called us, asking if you were here. He's been trying to get in touch with you.'

I did a double-take. 'Geoff Miller? As in the England selector?' I called the random number back.

'Steven, Ryan Sidebottom's gone down injured,' Geoff told me. 'Get your stuff together: you're flying to Bangladesh.'

It was the moment that every young sportsman dreams of, and I was barely halfway out of bed. I'd been glued to the TV six months previously as England won the 2009 Ashes, with

Stuart Broad running through the Australians at The Oval. Suddenly I was on my way out to join him – as well as other world-class players like Alastair Cook, Kevin Pietersen and Graeme Swann – on a full international tour. I knew my bowling had started to impress the right people, but I'd assumed there would be heaps of guys ahead of me in the pecking order. But it was me that England wanted to take a closer look at, and I had that tantalising combination of nerves and excitement as I packed my belongings and prepared to fly. I'd only been overseas a handful of times, and always on cricket tours; now I was being driven to Heathrow for a business-class flight to Dhaka.

It was the fulfilment of a dream formed at the cricket clubs where I had grown up. My dad used to play every weekend, and our social lives were at the club: Watford Town CC in my formative years, where the earliest photos are of me asleep on the pool table in the clubhouse, then Langleybury Cricket Club – for whom I played in the National Village Cup – thereafter, with a couple of seasons at West Herts CC in my late teens to play some more competitive cricket on a Saturday. It was never forced upon me; I just picked up a love for the sport along the way. I was always tall; as I developed and progressed, I was clearly taller than everyone else. I had a decent action for a kid, and gradually worked my way up through age-group teams at Hertfordshire.

At under-13s, I wasn't put forward for regional trials by Hertfordshire; I was devastated, but my dad's friend found a solution. Phil Evans, who was the team manager for South of England Under-13s, got in touch with the coach, Toby Radford, and said, 'There's this lanky kid who can bowl pretty quick. He might be a bit all over the place, but it's worth having a look at him.' I went to a trial at East Grinstead Cricket Club, near Crawley, and it went well. The next year, I was walking off the pitch at the English Schools Cricket Association festival at Oundle School, after playing for the South against the Midlands, and Toby came and intercepted me. He said, 'Finny, will you come and be on the first Middlesex Academy?'. He had just taken on that role after being an age-group coach for the ECB.

What I didn't realise was that Essex were waiting on the other side of the rope. People were talking about me by that stage, because I was tall and bowled quite quick. Toby said, 'We'd love you to come and be part of our age-group sides, and then see what happens.' My parents knew how much I loved cricket, and encouraged me to go for it. After all, what did I have to lose? The Middlesex indoor centre at Finchley was just down the M1. My Mum would drive me there and back every Tuesday and Thursday to go and train in a more professional environment. My dad didn't drive, so she sacrificed so much to make sure I could chase my dream, something I'll be eternally grateful for. There were then arguments between Middlesex and Hertfordshire, who didn't want to let me go, about which team I would represent at under-15 level. It went to a tribunal, but Middlesex won. The process felt over the top, but it was flattering to feel wanted. From that moment onwards, I was a Middlesex player.

Dad was a club cricketer, a left-arm quickie. Even now, people come up to me and say, 'You're Terry Finn's son. You were quick, but not as quick as he was.' He played for Hertfordshire and was asked to trial for the Middlesex Club and Ground, effectively a second team. But I think it's fair to say he didn't take it that seriously: he went out the night before for too many beers and ended up in Bedford instead of Borehamwood, where he lived. He was involved in a bad car accident when he was much younger where two people died; he snapped his left forearm among other complications and never had the same pace again. He doesn't talk about it. He's of that generation. Most of what I know about his cricket I got from speaking to Mum, or people who played with him.

Some parents, when they weren't far away from achieving something themselves, push their children incredibly hard to do it in their place. Thankfully, it was the complete opposite for me. My parents would support me: my dad would give me honest feedback – typically, 'that was all right', or 'that wasn't very good'. But they were never, ever pushy parents, telling me what I had to do to achieve my goals. They were never the ones saying, 'My son is good enough.' It was more, 'If they think he's good enough, then brilliant. If not, so be it.' They watched almost every game of cricket I ever played in the UK and I always loved picking them out in the crowd and waving while I was on the field.

My younger sister, Claire, and I had a very normal upbringing and went to a very normal school: Parmiter's in Watford. It can't have been easy for her. As Dad didn't drive, Mum ferried me everywhere and Claire often ended up having to come along too. She sacrificed a fair amount of her formative years to help me play cricket, without ever really having a say in the matter. Again, it's something that, as I've got older and I have less tunnel vision, I have really appreciated.

I've never liked playing up to the idea that I'm a working-class lad, but my background is different to a lot of England cricketers. Mum was a secretary before becoming a housewife and a cleaner after she had me, and Dad was a printer. He worked for the *Sun* and then the *Daily Mirror*, and would do long night shifts. There'd be weeks where I'd hardly see him because he'd be sleeping while I was heading into school, and then he'd be leaving the house to go to work just as I got home. Later on, whenever I made a back page, his mates would save copies for him, which he kept in a scrapbook filled with clippings.

There were no foreign holidays for my family, so when I was picked to play for England Under-16s in South Africa, it was the first time I'd flown. The furthest we'd gone was the Isle of Wight, let alone going to another country. The team weren't staying in fancy accommodation or anything like that, but I had my eyes opened. Right away I realised how much fun it was to travel, especially going away to play cricket with your mates. It was when we played at Newlands, the beautiful Test ground in Cape Town, that it really hit me how much I wanted to do this when I was older. But I still didn't think it was a serious possibility, let alone something I'd be doing in a few years' time.

You might think that being away with an England team would have been a big deal at school, but it never felt like it. I wasn't that confident as a young lad. I always stood out, quite literally – I had a very early growth spurt aged twelve, and shot up well beyond six foot – and the fact that I was always the tallest kid in the room made me self-conscious. I spent a long time pretending I was six feet seven inches not six feet eight inches, which somehow felt more normal. Mum would have to buy my trainers at least a size up, for fear I'd grow out of them too soon. I was pretty shy, too. I wasn't one of the super-popular kids at junior school, and at senior school I just tried to slip under the radar. I was never particularly successful with girls, either, and would never come back into the classroom after a tour feeling like a hero. Cricket wasn't a cool sport, but it was dominating my time and my social life:

almost all of my close friends were friends I'd made through cricket. It was a weird existence as a teenager.

The first time that I realised I had a real chance to make it was aged fourteen, in early 2004. Andrew Strauss had just made his England debut, and came to Finchley to face the academy bowlers in the nets ahead of a tour to the West Indies. He turned up with his England bag, and I thought, 'Fuck, I want that bag one day.' By then, I'd have been six foot five or six, and stick thin. But I bowled quick at him, and he tumbled over while getting out of the way of a bouncer. Jason Pooley, the assistant coach, was at the back, laughing. I remember his words vividly: 'Fucking hell, Strauss, you just got put on your arse by a fourteen-year-old!' It was so exciting. This was a guy who had already played for England, a rising star who was on the cusp of breaking into the Test team, and I was good enough to cause him serious problems, albeit in the indoor centre where bowling conditions are favourable. I suddenly realised that I wasn't as far away from that level as I had always assumed.

Just before my sixteenth birthday, John Emburey called me into his office at Finchley to offer me a contract with Middlesex. Embers was an old-school off-spinner whom my dad had watched playing Test cricket for England for years; now, my parents were taking calls from him as Middlesex coach, telling them that he was about to present their son with a three-year contract. It was only worth £180 a week initially, pro rata, to cover 2005 to 2007, but it was the most exciting thing that could have happened to me as a teenager: I could call myself a professional cricketer, and I had a window into becoming one full-time. I already knew that was what I wanted to do with my life.

Soon after, at sixteen years and forty-three days old, I

got asked to make my first-class debut, against Cambridge University. Billy Godleman, Stuart Poynter and I, the three youngsters in the squad, got a lift from Embers, driving at what felt like 110mph up the motorway. We were all filled with nervous excitement as we squeezed in among four cricket bags, and Embers was racing along to get to Cambridge in ample time the night before the game to have some dinner. I thought, 'Is this really what professional cricket is like?' But I bowled pretty well in front of Ed Smith and Jamie Dalrymple, who had both played for England, and Ben Hutton, the club captain. It was my first proper experience of being on the same level as professionals. When I'd bowled to Strauss, I was just meant to be giving him practice; now, I was sharing a dressing room with players who were effectively my equals.

I finished my GCSEs in the summer of 2005, and got three As and eight Bs – not bad after playing first-class cricket when I should have been revising. But that summer was altogether more memorable for another reason. I'd been conscious of previous Ashes series – waking up to see Matthew Hayden had scored yet another hundred while I'd been asleep – but the 2005 series was the first one that really grabbed my attention. I was properly gripped: how could you not be? The series ran into mid-September, and I'd started sixth form by the time Pietersen hit his 158 at The Oval. It was the first time that cricket had been on at school, and everyone was watching; we sat in the common room, on beanbags, with the big old TV showing Channel 4. Strauss scored two hundreds in that series; I'd been in the same indoor centre as him, the same dressing room, and he was out there winning the Ashes for England. But I have to make an admission: my main memories of the series involve Glenn McGrath.

McGrath was my hero. He was just the greatest. I loved

his arrogance, and that Australian attitude: I'm the best. We are better than you. So much better than you. We're going to beat you 5–0. When England hosted the 1999 World Cup, there was only one thing I wanted: a replica Australia shirt, bright yellow with green stars and stripes. My parents bought it for me, and it wound people up seeing me wear my Aussie kit down to the cricket club for training. I always wanted to emulate what McGrath did. He was tall, he bowled really upright and he got close to the stumps in his release. He had that natural angle into right-handers, and across the lefties, and I just loved everything about him. That's what I remember best about 2005: him bowling at Lord's from the Pavilion End, cleaning up Michael Vaughan when he misread the length, then nipping it down the slope to get Ian Bell.

The previous summer, McGrath had played for Middlesex for a few weeks as an overseas player. I went to watch him bowl against Yorkshire in a one-day game at Southgate, and walked around the ground to take in his performance from as many different angles as I could: from side-on, I saw his carry; from behind his arm, I saw the shape he was getting on the ball. As the game got tight, he bowled a no-ball; off the free hit, he cleaned the guy up with a perfect leg-stump yorker. I was in awe of him. I went up to Simon Cook, one of my academy coaches, after the game and asked him to get McGrath to sign my ticket. He said, 'I'll get you into the dressing room. Come and say hello and have a chat.' I refused. I idolised McGrath, and I was so scared of going in and speaking to him. I handed Simon my ticket stub and begged him to get it signed on my behalf. I still have it at home, buried away in a shoebox.

I'd always felt it was important to complete my education, and my parents encouraged me to take it seriously. You never know what might happen – injuries have ruined plenty of careers before they've started. I was around Middlesex's first-team squads and I felt like I might have a real chance of making it, but until you fully get your opportunity with a proper run of first-team games, you just can't tell. Teachers would say, 'You're getting paid to play cricket,' but I'd tell them it was £180 a week – or £240 a week from my second year with Middlesex. Thankfully, the school were flexible with me; they understood that I'd be away for a few weeks at a time. The headmaster, Brian Coulshed, loved cricket, which helped.

I sat some of my A-level papers at the British High Commission in Malaysia, during an England Under-19s tour; somehow I resisted the temptation to cheat with nobody watching me. I was always a goody two shoes. I had a place to read sports science at Loughborough, who gave me a reduced offer of three Bs – which I got, in English literature, sociology and PE – but 2007 turned into a breakthrough summer for me. I did well for England Under-19s against Pakistan, and was picked by Middlesex for a handful of Pro40 games and the County Championship run-in as well.

I played in our Pro40 promotion/relegation play-off against Northamptonshire at Southgate Cricket Club – the venue I had watched McGrath at three years previously – and caught an influential eye. It was a rare chance to play alongside Strauss; he hadn't yet become England captain, but it felt inevitable that he would one day. He took two catches off my bowling in the gully, and I was named player of the match after returning figures of 3 for 30 in my eight overs. It was Bob Willis – big scary Bob Willis from the TV – who chose me for that award, and all of a sudden I had an England legend talking me up as a really promising young bowler.

That made my next decision far easier. I had everything sorted for university – accommodation, finance for my student loan – but twenty-four hours before I went up to Loughborough, I pulled the plug on it. What was the harm in deferring for a year and seeing where I was in twelve months' time? I told them, 'I'm really sorry, but I can't do this. I'm going to try and become a professional,' and spent the winter training with Middlesex.

In late November, I walked into a hotel room in Chennai, which I was meant to be sharing with Chris Tremlett. I'd been called up to the England Performance Programme for a tour to India on the back of my performances for the Under-19s; it was a strong squad, with guys like Michael Carberry and Jonathan Trott, who had been excellent in first-class cricket and were serious contenders for the England team. India was a culture shock, not least when I found Tremlett – whom I'd watched bowl to Rahul Dravid and Sachin Tendulkar that summer – naked on all fours in the bathroom. He stuck out his hand and said, 'Hi, I'm Chris. Go and ask for another room, because whatever I've got, you don't want to catch it.' That was my introduction to Trem. I didn't know a human could make the noises he did that day.

I'd played three Championship games that year, taken 11 wickets and bowled OK, but I knew when I arrived in India that it would be a step up. We trained hard, and I was con-stantly aware of the fact that I was bowling to guys who were proper professionals; consistent performers, not just youngsters with a bit of promise like me. It was the first time I'd really experienced reverse swing, and I loved it straight away. It felt like I'd discovered an extra weapon that I didn't know I had, one that would make me far more dangerous away from home. I realised that I wasn't just cannon fodder for the guys in that squad; I held my own, and felt like I warranted my place on that tour, wearing an England tracksuit and training kit while rubbing shoulders with Test cricketers.

I'd experienced some pain in my groin though on this tour and it turned out to be my first trip into the operating theatre to have my body adjusted. I had a procedure called a Gilmore's groin, effectively a sports hernia, and at the same time had a realignment of my right adductor. The rehabilitation was frustrating but I always had in my mind that I wanted to be fit to play in the Under-19 World Cup in early 2008. It was an opportunity to test myself against my peers from around the world. I made it through the rehab, and shared a room with Chris Woakes throughout the trip to Malaysia. We became great mates, and still are to this day.

It was there that I had my first taste of playing cricket against Australia and feeling the rivalry that would define my career. We'd lost to an India side captained by Virat Kohli in the quarter-finals, and met the Aussies in the fifth-place play-off. There was nothing riding on it, but in one sense it was almost more intense than the real thing; everyone involved played up to what they thought an England vs Australia match should be like, based on what they'd seen on TV growing up. A couple of the Australians' best players – Phil Hughes and Steve Smith – went home to play in their domestic first-class competition, the Sheffield Shield, but they still had a strong team, which included Marcus Stoinis and James Faulkner. It's funny to look back on it, but we were all so fired up, and there was real aggression, with both teams getting into the battle and sledging each other. It gave me a sense of what could lie ahead of me – and I loved it.

That tournament was a who's who of international cricketers over the next decade. Kohli was on the cusp of playing for India, with Ravindra Jadeja as his vice-captain; Tim Southee made his Test debut a few weeks later, after playing for a New Zealand team captained by Kane Williamson and featuring Trent Boult and Corey Anderson; Imad Wasim and Umar Akmal were there for Pakistan, Dinesh Chandimal for Sri Lanka, and Darren Bravo for West Indies. I was playing with Liam Dawson, James Taylor and Woakes. I looked at my peers – guys I was competing well with – and all of a sudden they were playing international cricket and holding their own. It emphasised that I wasn't a million miles away from where I wanted to be.

That summer, I played twelve out of sixteen Championship games for Middlesex, and was starting to feel like I belonged. I missed two games early in the season when Vernon Philander arrived from South Africa as an overseas player, and, after a couple of quiet performances midway through, I was left out for two more. I was furious; it was the first time in my career that I'd been properly dropped from anything, be it youth sides or the second team. I took it terribly. I sulked, and was a complete drain for a few weeks. I didn't understand the feeling of being left out – particularly when I thought I should be playing – and didn't know how to process the sense of rejection that came with it. My overwhelming response was, 'Fuck you. You've got this wrong and I'm going to prove that to you.' There was no doubt in my mind that I should have been playing in those games.

It had been a tough period for the club, but it felt like things were on the up that summer. We finished third in Division 2 of the Championship, not far off promotion, and won a trophy – the Twenty20 Cup – for the first time in fifteen years. I'm still not sure why, but Daniel Radcliffe came into the dressing room to celebrate with us. Growing up, we would always try to catch a glimpse of him, Emma Watson or Rupert Grint when our school bus drove past Leavesden Studios, where Harry Potter was filmed; all of a sudden, I was having a beer with the main character. I only played a handful of T20 games, when our overseas players were unavailable, but winning the title meant we qualified for two further tournaments: the Stanford Super Series in Antigua, and the inaugural Champions League in India. University stopped being a consideration; I felt as though I was getting better all the time, and overtaking my peers with every few months that passed. I thought, 'This is my life now.'

It was in Antigua that I found myself in a full senior England dressing room for the first time. The tournament was the brainchild of Allen Stanford, with a centrepiece match for $20 million between England and West Indies, rebranded as the 'Stanford Superstars'. That probably told you all you needed to know about Stanford: a few months later, he was charged with running a Ponzi scheme and thrown in jail. As winners of our respective national competitions, Middlesex were up against Trinidad and Tobago, who outplayed us to take home $280,000; similar to the England team, we had meetings where people lost sight of the fact that we actually had to win the game to get the money and were squabbling about what their percentage cut was going to be. Stanford near enough treated us like pets, but we had a great time in Antigua on the beers for two weeks.

We were on the beach on the day of England's warm-up game against Trinidad and Tobago when our coaching staff heard there was an illness outbreak in the England camp. They were down to eleven fit players, so Dawid Malan and I were summoned as substitute fielders. It felt like an amazing opportunity: what if someone rolled an ankle in the warm-ups and I was suddenly playing? I walked into the dressing room and was in awe. I'd watched Kevin Pietersen and Andrew Flintoff on TV for years, pretended to be them in the nets; now I was on twelfth-man duties for them. It was my first actual glimpse into the England environment.

The only problem was that I had to take part in the fielding warm-ups, at a time when I was not a proficient fielder: very gangly, uncoordinated and not confident under the high ball. Even worse, the floodlights at Stanford's ground – next to the airport in Antigua – were so low that even the best fielders struggled to pick the ball up out of the night sky. Mark Garaway, one of England's assistant coaches, used his foam bat to biff high catch after high catch. It felt like I dropped almost every single one in that warm-up, in front of Pietersen and Flintoff. They must have thought, 'Is this bloke really a professional?' – but at least I could say that I'd been in an England dressing room and rubbed shoulders with the best players in the country. I was determined that it would be something I'd do again.

I woke early on the morning we were due to leave for the Champions League, ready to head to the airport, and quickly learned that the trip was off. We were scheduled to play Victoria, the Titans from South Africa and Chennai Super Kings, with our first fixture in Mumbai, but the city had been targeted in a terror attack the night before. England were already in India playing a one-day international (ODI) series, and later went back for two Tests, but there was speculation that some players might not feel safe to return. It was the first time that I read my name in the press linked with an England call-up: Tim Murtagh, Alan Richardson and I were the three fast bowlers outside of the squad with active Indian visas, and were supposedly on standby in case somebody pulled out. It would have been a strange situation, playing for my country almost by default and owing to a horrific situation after the attacks, but I couldn't help but feel excited when I saw my name in those reports.

Back at Middlesex, Angus Fraser's appointment as the club's director of cricket ahead of the 2009 season was a significant moment in my career – and in my life. Gus had been an England stalwart in the 1990s, and treated me like a son. It was a lovely relationship. We'd sit up on the high stools in the Long Room at Lord's while Middlesex were batting, or in the viewing gallery of the real tennis court at the back of the pavilion, and spend hours chatting about bowling. He took me under his wing; it was all about nurturing, rather than him telling me what I should be doing. He'd ask, 'What did that feel like?' or 'What did you think tactically to that opening bat?' You need a natural talent to play professional cricket, but to be successful at the top level, you have to learn about the intrinsic art of bowling. At that stage, I had largely been wanging it down there and hoping for the best; Gus helped me to understand the game's nuances.

He'd point things out about opposition bowlers, and ask me about them: 'He's moved wider on the crease there. Why has he done that?' If I didn't know, he'd explain: 'It's to try and take the batsman's head outside the line of off stump.' When I was standing at the top of my mark that season, I'd think, 'This is what we were talking about. I've bowled three balls that he's played and missed at; if I come wider on the crease, the natural angle will bring it back into him and he'll play all around it.' Gus was tactical, rather than technical, and that was the type of coaching that I responded to at that time. I was headstrong, and stubborn in the fact that I thought I was good. I had an inner confidence that what I was doing was right, and I was seeing progression, so I would try to implement whatever I'd been talking about with Gus.

I played fourteen out of sixteen Championship games that summer, and the games I missed were because I'd been rested, rather than dropped. That felt like a compliment: the club valued me so highly that they wanted me to be as fresh as possible. It was my breakthrough year: I was a regular in all formats, which felt like an achievement in itself, and Gus gave me my county cap at the end of the season. I signed a new five-year contract with Middlesex, and scraped together everything I had to buy my two-bed flat in Abbots Langley, for £172,000. I was starting to catch people's eye: I took 53 wickets in the Championship, and while I still felt as though I could happily slip under the radar, I started to develop a sense of confidence that I was doing well. I knew that I could bowl quick, and while I'd be quite introverted off the field – I wasn't a loud voice in the dressing room – I was uber-competitive on it. I always enjoyed having those fiery battles: I had a deep-rooted will to win when playing other sports growing up, and would never shy away from getting physical when I could.

One spell in particular stood out for me that summer, and made me confident that I was heading in the right direction. I was bowling to Chris Rogers – who would soon become my teammate, and later an Ashes rival – at Uxbridge. I knew he was one of the best players on the county circuit; he'd been scoring runs for fun for Derbyshire, and wasn't far away from the Australia team. I bowled with steep bounce and good pace on a placid pitch, and had him hopping around as the ball went flying past his left shoulder through to wicketkeeper John Simpson. It was another notch on the belt, as I proved to myself that I could compete with top players in county cricket.

I worked really hard that winter with Kevin Shine, the ECB's fast-bowling lead. I was picked for two tours by the England Lions, the national second-string team: red-ball in South Africa before Christmas, and white-ball in the UAE in the new year. I felt great. I cranked up the pace and knew I was bowling fast; Shiney loved using his handheld speed gun, and the numbers backed it up. It was a strong squad – Ian Bell was out there, trying to get back into the one-day team – and for me, it was another chance to show the guys I'd watched win the Ashes that summer that I could properly bowl.

In South Africa, we bowled to the full England team – who were there for a Test series – in the nets at Pretoria. I never liked bowling bouncers in the nets; I was still young and timid, and I didn't want to run the risk of hurting my teammates, especially guys preparing for a Test match. I bowled an un-impressive spell, bringing batters forward on to the front foot but never really testing them. Ajmal Shahzad had no such inhibitions. He sensed his opportunity to bowl as fast as he could, and was sending down bouncers, the ball whizzing past Pietersen's head. Andy Flower, the England coach, loved it: he saw Aj's talent and aggression and recognised his potential. He asked the Lions coaches for as much information as he could get on him, and picked him for the white-ball squads soon after. I'm not sure he even noticed me; I felt totally invisible.

It meant that when we arrived in Abu Dhabi to play a T20 against the full England team, I was determined to impress Flower and make him look in my direction. England were pre-paring for the World T20 in the Caribbean, but we rolled them over: I took 2 for 25 from my four overs, bounced Joe Denly out, and then watched Michael Lumb and Craig Kieswetter smack the England bowlers everywhere. This time, I knew that

I had caught Flower's eye. I thought, 'If anything happens to anyone here, my name is going to be in vogue as a possible replacement.' Little did I know that one month later, I'd be making my Test debut.

# 2

# Making Strides

'We've got a warm-up game tomorrow,' Andy Flower told me as I walked into the England team hotel in Chittagong, Bangladesh, 'and I want you to play in it.'

'Fuck it,' I thought. 'What have I got to lose?' I was twenty years old, five thousand miles from home, and even further away from my comfort zone. If it went well, I could impress the guys I'd watched and admired from afar and prove to them that I was a serious bowler. If not, I could blame the jet lag and shrug it off in the knowledge that I had my whole career ahead of me. It was this mindset that allowed me to feel totally free: a mindset that you chase for the rest of your career in the hope that you can approach things with the same gay abandon.

The journey out to Bangladesh was the first time in my life that I'd flown business class. I got to the lounge and thought, 'Jesus, this is all right,' as I loaded up on free food. Changing planes in Dhaka, I stumbled across Eoin Morgan, my Middlesex teammate and one of my closest friends; he was flying home after the ODI series, where he'd made his maiden England hundred. We barely had time to catch up, but it was nice to see a familiar face halfway across the world. The connecting flight took me to Chittagong, where the opportunity of a lifetime lay waiting for me. I was less enamoured with the aircraft that flew me internally, a propeller plane that shook all the way there; by the time I landed, all the blood had drained from my face.

I met my new teammates briefly at breakfast on the morning of the game and was overwhelmed by nerves. I wasn't bad in social situations, but I felt myself become shy and insular to the extent that I couldn't drag myself back up to the breakfast bar for a second helping of eggs on toast. I had a sense of imposter syndrome: I knew I was a left-field call-up, because my stats for Middlesex were OK without being anything special. I'd watched these players winning the Ashes the previous summer, but I'd barely met any of them in real life and assumed none of them would have a clue who I was. It was only when they started coming up to me and introducing themselves that I began to settle down.

We bowled first in the warm-up game, and everything went to plan. I bowled with a reverse-swinging ball, and felt like I did myself justice: 2 for 13 from my seven overs on the first day, both caught behind by Matt Prior. I had felt like I'd embarrassed myself in front of Kevin Pietersen eighteen months previously, dropping all those high catches in Antigua, but now he was impressed: 'That's proper reverse-swing bowling,' he said. There is nothing better than bowling with a ball that is reversing; even after my retirement, the one thing that would make me want to get a pair of spikes on would be the chance to bowl with a reverse-swinging ball. I'd find the energy. It provided me with an opportunity to attack, and I knew it suited my strengths. The chance to wreak havoc gave me such pure excitement. You have a greater margin for error when the ball is reversing, which lends itself to that feeling of being free: you have to fully commit to what you are doing in order to get the ball to reverse, a mindset that I could seize whenever I was presented with the conditions for it. I spent years chasing that feeling later in my career as I made my way back from my lowest, darkest moments.

Stuart Broad had been rested, and I knew that I'd outbowled the seamers who'd been selected for the tour initially – including Ajmal Shahzad, whose performance in that Pretoria nets session had earned him a call-up. I took 1 for 20 from eleven overs in the second innings, providing the control that I knew Flower cherished. I had a quiet hope that I might have done enough to get in the team, but figured they would likely stick with the established pecking order. Immediately afterwards, my main focus was on my body, which was cramping from my feet up to my shoulders – a combination of excitement, jet lag and bowling in serious heat and humidity. I was on the physio bed in the dressing room with four blokes stretching me out, and everyone was pointing at me and laughing. Every time I moved, a different part of my body started to cramp; I'd try to turn to look at someone, and all of a sudden, my neck had gone. The pain was seriously uncomfortable, but proved that I'd left nothing out there on the pitch.

You don't realise it at the time, but your mindset as a young player is as free as it will ever be. In spite of my nerves, I threw myself into that match, never doubting that I would be good enough to compete against a second-string Bangladesh team. I knew there was a world where I wouldn't be ready for international cricket yet, but I had the talent and the skill. If I bowled a pile of shit, then I'd have another fifteen years to have a crack at it. My career path had been tracking up the whole time; there was no doubt in my mind that I'd be ready to play for England at some stage. If it wasn't now? So be it. The consequences weren't important. If I'd been smashed, I'd have shrugged my shoulders and said, 'I'm twenty! What were you expecting?' And when I did as well as I did, my confidence became sky-high.

Alastair Cook was stand-in captain for the Test series – Andrew Strauss had been rested – and he pulled me aside just after practice the day before the first Test. 'You're in,' he told me. 'You're going to make your Test debut tomorrow.' Michael Atherton gave me my cap – along with Michael Carberry, who also made his debut – and we batted first. I was down in my usual role at number 11, which meant that I spent my first day as a fully fledged England cricketer with my feet up in the dressing room. Cricket is a strange sport in that sense, particularly for us bowlers: you spend so much of the time off the field that you can't possibly watch every ball of a match you're involved in, especially a five-day Test match. As Cook batted through the day against Bangladesh's spinners, I lay there watching episodes of *The Inbetweeners* that I'd downloaded on my iPhone. Graeme Swann let me control the music briefly, so I stuck on the song I'd been listening to on repeat on the flight over: 'Tomorrow in the Bottle', by Timbaland and Chad Kroeger from Nickelback. Swanny took one look at me and said, 'Never again.' My lime-green iPod ended up out of the dressing-room window. I was still working my new teammates out: most of them didn't play much county cricket, so I'd only met them in passing. I wasn't intimidated or overawed, just wide-eyed. I'd gone from having a solid domestic season, playing in Division 2, to playing with the guys I'd watched on TV. I thought, 'This has escalated very fucking quickly.'

We declared on the second day, and moments before we went out to field, I sent my mum a text. This was just before the ICC's anti-corruption team took phones off you as you walked into the dressing room, but I couldn't get any service on my iPhone in any case, so I was using an old-school brick. I wrote something like: *Just going out to field now in my first Test match*, but Flower caught me. 'Finn!' he yelled at me. 'Put that fucking phone down! You're playing international fucking sport!' He ran a tight ship in that England team. I must have said sorry ten times in two seconds before running down on to the pitch.

My first ball in an England shirt went for four: Tamim Iqbal, the Bangladesh opener, flicked it around the corner to fine leg. I'd gone into that warm-up match with an amazing mentality, but by now I was desperate to make the most of my opportunity. I was harsh on myself; every time I walked back to the top of my mark after being hit for a boundary, I was chuntering and berating myself. At the time, I thought it was normal: I was playing international sport with some amazing players – greats of the game. Those were the standards I expected from myself. That was very much the language of the team: keeping high standards, always being switched on mentally and making sure you weren't lazy. It meant that even in my first spell in international cricket, I was incredibly self-critical. Perhaps it was a warning sign, or a window into the perfectionism that I chased as my career progressed. What's wrong with striving for perfection, right? That was what all the sportsmen I had admired had done from a young age; why shouldn't I be the same?

I took my first Test wicket on the third morning – the nightwatchman, Shahadat Hossain, caught at second slip by Paul Collingwood – and struck again in the second innings, nicking off opener Imrul Kayes. I took one wicket in each innings of the second Test, too, and finished the series with four wickets at an average of 44 in conditions that could hardly have suited me less. We won both Tests in spin-friendly conditions – Swann took 16 wickets – and while I'd been self-critical at times, the bigger picture was wholly positive. I felt quietly accepted by the dressing room for being able to bowl at that level, and that was all I wanted. I didn't feel like I was destined to play a hundred Test matches, but nor did I feel out of my depth. Clearly I knew there would be tougher challenges to come than Bangladesh – who had some good players, but had hardly won a Test – but I had the respect of guys whose opinions I valued. With James Anderson coming back from a rest, I realised that I might not start the summer in the team, but I'd had a good first taste of Test cricket.

The second Test in Dhaka gave me an insight into the intensity of the top level – and an idea of the attention to detail expected within the England environment under Flower. I was fielding at fine leg, not far away from Jonathan Trott, when the ball was hit towards him at deep backward square. Trott ran in off the boundary, picked it up and threw it to the keeper's end on the bounce. We were trying to get the ball reversing, keeping one side shiny and the other roughed up, but Trotty's throw landed on the shiny side, an awkward distance away from Prior. From nowhere, Prior unleashed hell, sending a volley of abuse out towards Trott sixty-five metres away. Trotty wasn't having it and swore back at him; for the next two overs, they were screaming at one another. I'd never seen anything like it before, and as I stifled my laughter at two grown men arguing about a throw, I realised how high the standards were that I would be expected to meet as an international cricketer. Indirectly, it gave me a kick up the backside and prompted me to work incredibly hard on my fielding with Richard Halsall, one of Flower's assistant coaches, over the next couple of years.

The small things that came along with playing at the top level added some additional motivation for me. The night before we travelled from Chittagong to Dhaka for the second Test, I was told to leave my bags outside my hotel room; we arrived at the next hotel after a flight and they were already there, as if by magic. I was used to lugging kitbags and suitcases through airports on overseas tours, but this was a completely different world to anything I'd experienced before. But all the perks were just a bonus; the main thing was being out on the pitch wearing an England badge on my chest. I never felt like I was destined to play at that level, or as though I deserved it. Instead, it was something that I deeply wanted to do, and had worked bloody hard to make happen – as had other people in my life. My parents had sacrificed a lot for me: Mum had driven me halfway across the country to and from matches, and Dad had come along to watch me play when he should have been sleeping around long overnight shifts. I was always desperate to make them proud, right the way through my career.

Playing for my country was an incredibly special moment. But when I got home from Bangladesh, I knew the stakes had gone up. Before the start of the 2010 season, Middlesex had a training day at the National Performance Centre in Loughborough, where I didn't feel in good rhythm. My response was to throw a massive tantrum: I chucked a ball at the side of the indoor centre and embarrassed myself in front of my teammates. I felt like shit; I knew I couldn't blow my opportunity to play for England again, because I'd had that taste. Little did I know that Broad would be resting for the first Test of the summer – again, against Bangladesh – and so I felt like I was competing with him, Anderson, Tim Bresnan, Graham Onions, Liam Plunkett, Ryan Sidebottom, Shahzad...

the list was endless. I had to do absolutely everything in my power to make that place in the team my own. Anything else went out of the window.

I was utterly single-minded; cricket had taken over my life. Early that season, my grandad – on my mum's side of the family – passed away. He loved cricket, and although he sadly never watched me play for England in the flesh, I was grateful that he lived long enough to know I'd made my Test debut. On the day he died, I trained at Radlett Cricket Club with Andrew Strauss; it was an England-specific session, geared around me bowling to him. I broke down in tears in the dressing room afterwards, and when Strauss came over to check on me, I told him what had happened. 'So what the fuck are you bowling to me for?' he replied. I knew deep down that I shouldn't have been there; I should have been with my family, supporting them and processing the grief. But I was desperate to make the most of the opportunity to bowl to the England captain and make him realise that I deserved to be playing in the first Test of the summer. That was just the way my head worked: I wanted to work as hard as I possibly could to push myself forward and achieve my dreams.

Strauss was at first slip for Middlesex for our opening Championship fixture against Worcestershire at New Road. I've rarely bowled better: I took five wickets in the first innings, then nine in the second. It should have been ten; the only batsman I didn't dismiss was Phil Jaques, and I had him dropped by Strauss. I still haven't forgiven him! My match figures were 14 for 106, the best of my career. Even though we – somehow – managed to lose, I felt like I was inching closer to selection in the first Test. But I was so obsessed with the idea of proving myself, and making good on this opportunity, that I lost sight of the bigger picture: while the rest of my family were at my grandad's funeral, I was bowling against Northamptonshire at Wantage Road, getting carved around by Stephen Peters. I thought, 'If I miss this match and Bresnan takes six-for, I'm fucked.' Even after taking 14 wickets in a match, all I told myself was, 'That's not enough.' One of my cousins sent me a text that night, making very clear what they thought of my decision to skip the funeral to play a game of county cricket. I've always regretted it, but I bet there are countless athletes out there with similar stories. You can lose all perspective on life as your game becomes your whole world.

Come the end of May, I was in the side for the first Test against Bangladesh. It was incredibly special: it was my first Test in England, my first at Lord's, my home ground, and I was playing alongside Eoin, who was making his Test debut. We were both so excited to be playing at Lord's together, and there's a great photo of us underneath the honours board with the dressing-room attendant, Pete Lowe, who'd been there for us when we were playing for Middlesex. My dad doesn't travel overseas – he's never had any interest in flying – and going to Bangladesh at a week's notice was a non-starter for my mum, so this was the first time they had watched me playing for England. I remember looking over and seeing them in the family box in the Tavern Stand. Coming so soon after Grandad had died, I cherished the feeling of making my parents proud.

I took nine wickets in the match, including 5 for 87 in the second innings, to get my name up on the honours board. I'd been looking at that board ever since I first walked into the Lord's dressing room as a sixteen-year-old, and was pinching myself that my name would be up there. It was a real achievement, a month after my twenty-first birthday and in my first home Test, but nothing satisfied me. At that stage, that attitude suited me; I was chasing constant improvement, never wanting to stand still, and soaking up new information all the time. But it meant that I hardly acknowledged my success: that night, rather than celebrating with the rest of the squad in London, I was back at my flat, sitting on the sofa on my own with a large pepperoni pizza and some chicken dippers from Domino's. I've always known how to treat myself. I'd convinced myself that was the right way to approach international sport: never resting on your laurels. I was already thinking ahead to the second Test in Manchester.

And so, I somehow convinced myself that my performance wasn't good enough. 'I should have taken 5 for 20,' I thought. 'It's embarrassing to be on the honours board with 5 for 87. I need to do better next time around.' I was already chasing that perfect five-for; in my head, I wanted it to be against Australia, not Bangladesh. It felt like the pursuit of perfection was not just the right approach, but the only one worth having. I didn't allow myself to stop and reflect on the positives of what I was doing; even when almost everything was going right, I wasn't allowing myself to enjoy these moments. It seemed to work well early on, when my trajectory was only heading in one direction, but it meant I ingrained bad habits: unless something was flawless, I was never happy and took it out on myself. I'd taken nine wickets in my first home Test, but could only focus on the fact that I'd gone at nearly four runs per over.

I took another five-for in the second Test in Manchester, and was named England's player of the series – not that you'd have known it from my interview at the post-match presentation. 'The other guys bowled a lot better than me,' I said. 'I bowled better at Lord's and there are a lot of areas to improve; going at more than four an over is not ideal, really, in a Test match...' I've bowled too many four balls, and been a bit loose.' I'd taken 15 wickets in the series, six more than anyone else, but I wasn't satisfied.

Playing in the second Test earned me an incremental England contract, and I didn't play another game for six weeks. Instead, the ECB put me on a 'strengthening programme' – which was essentially heaps of gym work, because I was still as skinny as a twig. I wasn't happy with it because I just wanted to play cricket; Angus Fraser's attitude was: 'If you are in rhythm and taking wickets, don't waste it.' But the long-term goal was that I would become fit enough and strong enough to be available for five Ashes Tests later in the year. David Warner, the Australian opener, who had started to make his name in international cricket, was playing T20 for Middlesex that summer, and we developed a good relationship. I wasn't allowed to play, so we'd often be out on the town together. He was outspoken about it in the press, saying it was 'ridiculous' that I was lifting weights and doing sprints when I should have been bowling. With everything that was to come in our respective careers, it's funny to think that a young David Warner would be sticking up for his English mate.

I was disappointed not to be involved in the one-day squad, but my fitness work was organised around England's schedule, and I was often in the dressing room. It meant I continued to get a sense of Andy Flower's coaching style, and his desire for control both on the pitch and off it. In an ODI at Lord's, Shaun Tait was bowling thunderbolts for Australia to our top order. Pietersen had got injured in our fielding innings, and Michael Yardy was padded up waiting to go in at number 3 and face Tait. He looked like he'd rather be anywhere else in the world. Flower walked through the dressing room on his way to watch from the balcony, and said, 'I don't want to hear a single word from anyone about how quick Shaun Tait is bowling.' Ajmal

Shahzad missed the memo, because he had been over on the Nursery Ground having a bowl and came back just in time to see *100.1mph* flash up on the big screen. 'Bloody hell, that's fucking rapid, like!' he said, only to look around and see half the dressing room glaring at him and the other half laughing. Thankfully Flower was elsewhere, otherwise Aj would have copped an earful.

We beat Pakistan 3–1 to close out the summer, and I started to feel like I belonged in Test cricket. In my mind there wasn't any question as to whether I would be playing in that series. Pakistan were a step up from Bangladesh; I loved the feeling of getting top players out, especially with proper fast bowler's dismissals, nipping the ball away and having batters well caught at second slip or in the gully. Eoin kept his place, with Ian Bell injured, and we had a lot of fun together, enjoying each other's success. At Trent Bridge, he hit a straight six to reach his maiden Test hundred; I was watching from a viewing gallery directly behind the bowler's arm. We celebrated with a mountain of chicken wings and beers at Hooters in Nottingham; it was proper schoolboy stuff, and we were two young guys living the dream.

I was still self-critical, but playing for England gradually gave me a sense of confidence that I'd never experienced before. I wasn't fully satisfied by any means, but I realised that the rewards I was getting – positive articles in the newspapers, a sponsored car and, at the end of the summer, a central contract – were proof that I was tracking upwards all the time. I'd always been interested in watches and bought myself an Omega Seamaster during the Pakistan series. I walked into the shop, picked it out, and left thinking, 'Fucking hell, I just paid for a two-grand watch on my card. This is mad!' I had a three-door Mercedes, which I thought was pretty fancy, and would see my teammates arriving in five-litre supercars through England's sponsorship deal with Jaguar. (I got my hands on one later that summer – which I promptly managed to write off on the one-way system in Watford a few months later.) I was focused on my cricket first and foremost, but of course there was an aspirational aspect alongside it – especially as a young guy who hadn't had the means to treat himself like that before.

Eoin had an amazing ability to deal with the press. He's three years older than me, so was a little bit more worldly, and would tell me, 'Just remember, you're never as amazing as they say you are, and you're never anywhere near as bad as they say you are. You're always somewhere in the middle.' When he caught me looking at something about myself on my phone or in the paper, he used to ask me why I was bothering to read that stuff. I was in the midst of an early peak in my career, so I was loving it. You feel invincible when you're that age and only ever reading nice things about yourself; I would sit down for an interview with a journalist and they'd write a glowing piece about me. But there were plenty of troughs to follow on the way, and if I'd been as level-headed as Eoin about the scrutiny that comes with international cricket, maybe I'd have been better equipped to manage them. A little bit of extra experience and maturity can go a long way in a very short career.

I had bowled well at Lord's in the final Pakistan Test, and in the first innings I got Umar Akmal out with one of the best balls I'd bowled in an England shirt: a reverse-swinging yorker that sneaked under the bat and crashed into his off stump. But that night, the News of the World broke the story that some of Pakistan's players had been caught in a spot-fixing sting, and suddenly we started to second-guess everything that we had achieved in the series. They had beaten us at The Oval, and Mohammad Amir, one of the players implicated, had bowled amazingly through the series, but it made us question everything.

It was a surreal final day at Lord's: we didn't celebrate any of the wickets when we bowled them out, and everything felt weirdly flat. There had been the odd suspicion that something wasn't quite right. I'd been in the dressing room looking at the TV replays of Amir's huge no-ball, wondering how on earth anyone could get it that wrong, but I thought the other lads were just being cynical when they said, 'He must be on the take.' As it turned out, they were spot on: Amir, Mohammad Asif and Salman Butt were all banned for five years, and even spent time in jail. The bigger picture, though, was that we'd ticked off another important step on the way towards the Ashes series, which was now staring us in the face. With every day that passed, it became more of a reality that I'd be there playing a part in it.

I'd never been to Australia before, and was prepared for the absolute worst. England had lost the last series there 5–0 in 2006/07, and all the players who had been on that tour told me, 'This is as hard as it gets. Be ready for the toughest experience of your life.' That was only reinforced by our pre-tour boot camp. We turned up at the airport with no idea where we were going or what we were doing beyond 'team building', so when our boarding passes said *Munich* on them, we thought, 'Brilliant, Flower is sending us to Oktoberfest.' When we landed, we were met off the plane by some Australians with buzz cuts, who looked like they meant business. 'Phones and contraband in the bag,' they said. Everyone looked at each other, confused, and reluctantly gave up their phones, wallets and anything else they had on them. I even had to give up my two packs of Tangfastics. We were dropped off in the woods in the middle of nowhere, and realised that these guys were military types who were not messing around.

What followed was three days of hell. The first night we were there, we'd been marching through the Bavarian forest all day, each carrying two bricks, which we were told would be our 'best friends' for the next three days. The policy was no first names or nicknames: if someone said 'Chris' or 'Trem' instead of 'Mr Tremlett', the whole group would be told to get down and do fifty press-ups with heavy backpacks on. Paul Collingwood was the first to break the rule, about a minute into the hike, and was forced to stand at the front and count everyone's press-ups for them. The mantra was that if you messed up, you got everyone else punished.

We pitched our tents, exhausted from carrying our new best friends around all day, and woke barely an hour later to cries of, 'Out, out, out!' with torches shining in our faces. We were told we had ninety seconds to be standing around the campfire, and then we were straight off again, half dressed, on a run through the forest. Monty Panesar was pleading with the instructors, saying, 'We are not animals!' The Australians were shouting back, 'It's 10.30 a.m. in Brisbane, fellas, the first ball is in two months. That means it's go-time! You've got to be ready for anything!' I was thinking, 'Yeah, but it's the middle of the night in Bavaria and it's fucking freezing. I hope it's a bit nicer than this in Brisbane.'

I was so naive. I just assumed this must be what happened before an Ashes series in Australia, so I copped it and got on with it. The idea was that shared hardship would bring us closer together; that going through something unbelievably difficult as a team would mean that if things got tough in Australia, we'd have a collective experience to fall back on.

But even Flower realised by the end that it probably went a bit over the top. The human element of it was good, at least. On the last night, we sat around the campfire begging the blokes for boiling water for our powdered nasi goreng sachets, and went round the group answering the question: 'What does it mean to you to be going to the Ashes?' I told everyone about my grandad passing away; Pietersen explained how becoming a father that year had changed his priorities. Then again, some parts of it were definitely unnecessary, like the boxing bouts they set up – Tremlett was so strong that a punch he landed on Jimmy ended up breaking one of his ribs – while Alastair Cook missed the whole thing because he was at his brother's wedding. At least my boxing match wasn't much of a contest. I was paired with Monty, who had given up before we started; he went limp and didn't throw a single punch.

It was Gus who advised me to keep a diary in Australia. He'd played in three away Ashes series during England's long run without a series win Down Under – which stretched back to 1986/87 – and tried to help me manage my expectations. Like everyone else, he told me it would be very difficult: in English cricket, Australia was where careers and reputations got ruined, and everybody was wary of that happening to me at the age of twenty-one. Gus's suggestion was that using a journal would help me to keep in check all the emotions that would go on inside my head over the course of three months on the other side of the world.

The way that everyone talked it up, I thought there would be twenty thousand Australians waiting for us at the airport, hurling abuse and ready for a brawl, but when we actually got there, dressed in our team suits, I think the people on the other side of the plane door may have even smiled. The officers at the gate as we approached asked us to get all our cricket boots out of our kitbags, and we had to scrub the dirt off the soles to make sure we weren't bringing any outside soil into the country. Once we got past them, and had the customary TV cameras in our face for a few minutes as we boarded the team bus, we were off and running.

I'd spent most of the Bangladesh trip at cricket grounds or in hotel rooms, so Australia felt like my first opportunity to tour properly as an England player, experiencing an amazing country, going out for drinks and dinner and socialising with my teammates. Even though I put pressure on myself, and knew how big the series was for the team, I arrived with a positive attitude. I knew deep down that this would be a win-win situation for me: it was my first Ashes series, and nobody expected me to win it for England on my own; plus we'd been hammered last time, so just being competitive would represent an improvement. It almost felt like it would be a reconnaissance mission for me for the rest of my career, to get a taste of the Ashes and to see what Australia was like.

On our first night in Perth, Eoin and I had dinner with a good friend. I'd first met Billy Godleman at our South of England Under-13s trial, and we were like peas in a pod growing up. He was in Australia playing grade cricket, but as kids he was the player everyone wanted to be: a strong personality who grew up in north London and was not someone you'd fuck around with. He took me under his wing, and we were inseparable at the Middlesex Academy. Billy had a lot of success at a very young age: he scored mountains of runs at age-group level for England and made a century on his Championship debut aged seventeen. It helped me that I was in his slipstream. Everyone talked about him as the next big thing, and although we were best mates, I was always a rung below him. It was only when he left for Essex at the end of 2009 that I became the one in the spotlight. As it turned out, he never quite kicked on as people had expected. He played a lot of first-class cricket, but was never in the mix for England. It just goes to show that very few sporting careers turn out exactly as planned, and was probably a good reminder to me of just how lucky I was to be in the position I was.

We'd had a settled team for most of the summer, but the early weeks of the tour felt like everyone was jostling for spots. I was desperate to play in the first Test, but was fighting with Tim Bresnan and Tremlett for the fourth bowling slot. I knew I was the favourite, but I was well aware after jumping the queue in Bangladesh that one day's bowling could put someone else ahead of me. I was getting used to conditions and working out how to be effective on Australian pitches, and we approached our warm-up games with a much higher intensity than usual. The feeling from the guys who had been here before was that if we started by losing to – or even not winning convincingly against – a state team, we'd already be on the back foot with the press and the Australian public. There was a clear plan to treat the warm-ups seriously, and for the team to stay within our own bubble: it was us against the world.

We beat a strong Western Australia XI, and I picked myself up from a poor start to bowl far better as the game went on. *Bowled a shit first spell*, I wrote in my diary after the first day. *Being nailed in the press. Will have to get used to it. Not everything will go my way*. It was a sign of things to come that I was going back to the hotel and reading what people were saying about me in the media rather than blocking it out and relying on my coaches, my teammates and my own instincts for self-analysis. Much as Morgs told me that I shouldn't pay attention to it, curiosity would always get the better of me.

On the second evening, I had my confidence back after a good start to the second innings; and on the third, I wrote: *Best I've bowled in an England shirt today. Got praise from everyone about it. Really happy with pace.* I played all right in the second match, too, without bowling the house down, and we headed down to Hobart feeling confident. We were there for one final warm-up, but first we put the travelling UK press pack through their paces in the nets. We cranked up the pace on the bowling machines, threw catches off the catching ramps as fast as we could, and even had a few of them running between the wickets fully padded up. It was a window into the intensity of our training sessions for them, and gave a lot of the boys satisfaction to see the touring journalists hot and bothered in the indoor centre.

Rather than playing in the final warm-up, I was dispatched to Brisbane along with Anderson, Broad, Swann and our bowling coach, David Saker, to prepare for the first Test. I knew then that I would be playing at the Gabba, and started to appreciate the magnitude of what I was stepping into.

In the days leading up to the series, there were paparazzi waiting outside the hotel; it took me a moment to appreciate that *we* were the guests they wanted to photograph. I felt nervous about the prospect of playing in the Ashes for the first time, inevitably, but they were good nerves: a sense of excitement rather than fear. At times like that, anticipation pulses through your veins like electricity, imagining the possibilities. Later in my career I would battle with those feelings of anxiety and worry about the worst-case scenario; now, I could only see the positives. My entire cricketing career – in some ways my entire life – had been leading up to this moment, and I felt ready for it. But I also had the liberating mindset that I was doing things ahead of time: I had never expected to be in this position at the age of twenty-one, and it felt like an opportunity to lay the foundations for the rest of my career. There was a thrill about the chance to play at the Gabba, too; it was that much bigger than any of the grounds I'd played at back home, and I knew the noise and atmosphere would be incredible for the start of an Ashes series. We could sense how many English people had travelled over to follow us, and we were ready to do them proud.

**24 November 2010**

One day to go to the biggest test of my life so far. Excited at the prospect. Good training session, wicket with my first ball. Bowled Cooky. Fuller length here, but not floaty and has to be into the wicket. Know my plans to each batsman. Ground is incredible and the buzz is awesome. Can't wait to play in front of so many people. Relaxed with Morgs in eve and chilled. It's 11.11 and I'm struggling to sleep. Get my nut down soon and clear my head. Tomorrow will be AMAZING.

# 3

# Ashes Ambition

The moment that summed up my first Ashes series came in a Melbourne hotel room on the evening of 29 December 2010. It was the night of one of England's greatest wins over Australia: a total drubbing, by an innings and 157 runs, to take a 2–1 lead and retain the urn ahead of the fifth Test in Sydney. I had played a decent hand in the series: at that stage, only Jimmy Anderson (17) had taken more wickets than me (14). And yet I felt like an imposter during our celebrations. I'd been dropped for the fourth Test because I was conceding too many runs, too quickly, and found it really hard to process. I spent Boxing Day moping around as twelfth man, and was convinced that I had let a huge opportunity to prove myself at the top level pass me by. While the team were celebrating in the hotel, I went to my room to change and took long enough that Alastair Cook came to drag me back out. 'You're coming downstairs,' he told me. 'You're as much a part of this as everyone else.' But the truth is, I didn't feel it, because I hadn't been out there in the middle in the crucial Test match. I found it so hard to take a step back and look at the bigger picture.

Mind you, the idea that we would be 2–1 up heading into the final Test felt a long way off after three balls of the first one in Brisbane. We chose to bat first, and I wanted to take in the spectacle of an Ashes Test match, so I went out to watch the first over of the series. I had started to get used to playing in front of decent crowds during our home Test summer, but there were more than 35,000 in at the Gabba, stomping their feet and slamming their chairs. It felt like the stand was going to collapse in on us. The crowds I'd played in front of in England were quite sedate and polite, clapping the opposition when they hit a boundary or reached a landmark, but the Aussies were partisan and smelled blood. Third ball, Andrew Strauss guided Ben Hilfenhaus straight to Mike Hussey in the gully. The place went bananas. I'd never heard anything like it before; celebrating a Watford goal at Vicarage Road didn't even begin to compare. I thought, 'I'm not going to watch any more of this.' For the rest of our two batting innings, I sat in the dressing room, watching our guys on TV rather than with my own eyes as I tried to detach myself from the magnitude of what was going on.

It's only when you're actually at a Test match that you realise the length of the delay on satellite TV. The pictures we saw in the changing room were a few seconds behind what was happening out on the field, so you'd hear the commotion from the stands before you knew what had gone on. When Peter Siddle took his hat-trick, it was total bedlam. The whole concrete complex of the stadium shook and the fans went wild, and it was a scramble for the lower order to get their kit on in time. I had a bit more time than most since I was in at number 11, but Graeme Swann and Jimmy were both climbing over people to try and get padded up as the wickets tumbled to the backdrop of the Aussie supporters going nuts. It was a proper introduction to Ashes cricket, and gave me a clear sense of how much of a step up this was from playing against Bangladesh and Pakistan.

The game was bloody hard. We were behind for the entirety of the first three days: all out for 260, then out in the field for nearly 160 overs as they racked up a first-innings lead of 121. Hussey and Brad Haddin, the Australian wicketkeeper, both scored hundreds and put on a stand of over 300. Haddin let me know what he thought of me too.

**27 November 2010**

Long, hard day. Ended up with six-for, but didn't really deserve it. Too many four balls. Haddin getting stuck into me. Every time I passed him, he'd tell me I was shit or cack. Fair enough, I hadn't bowled well. Enjoyed bowling after tea. Nice to get Hussey and enjoyed Swanny getting Haddin. Great thing about the team is the unity. Everyone went hard at Haddin. It's up to me to concentrate better at finishing overs.

We had a lot of fun in that dressing room. The Black Eyed Peas released a song that year called 'The Time (Dirty Bit)', which got played whenever we were about to head into the field. The Gabba is set up so that the Australians would effectively walk past our rooms and straight out on to the pitch; we'd wait until the beat dropped and then all come bouncing out of the dressing room past them. Their batters looked at us like we were completely mental, but it showed there was still a quiet confidence that we were alive in the series, even though we'd had a tricky start.

I didn't want anyone to think I was a grass, but during one interval I did tell Kevin Pietersen and Matt Prior – who got along very well at the time – that Haddin was getting stuck into me whenever he passed me. I said, 'Look, it's not getting to me, but I'm just telling you.' At the start of the next session,

Pietersen and Prior walked Haddin to the middle, letting him have it from both barrels.

'You're brave, mate, picking on a 21-year-old.'

'You've got a big mouth, averaging thirty-odd in Test cricket.'

'Mate, you are fucking shit.'

It didn't make much difference to Haddin – he made 136, and still sprayed me – but the fact that those guys had my back made me feel like a valued part of the team. It sounds quite primitive and simple, but I really appreciated the fact that once the whole team clocked it, that us-against-them mentality came out. It would have been easy for the guys to say, 'Well, that's Ashes cricket for you,' and tell me to get on with it, but they wanted to have my back, which helped me manage and deal with it.

It's part of my psychological make-up that I am always chasing absolute perfection. I'd taken six-for in my first innings against Australia, on Ashes debut, but my focus was on the fact that it was 6 for 125 when I wanted it to be 6 for 25. Everyone went around the park, and I bowled more than thirty overs, but I felt a bit embarrassed to have gone at 3.7 an over. I'd taken a couple of big wickets on the second day – a sharp caught and bowled off Simon Katich for my first Ashes wicket, and a short ball to get Michael Clarke – but I knew I'd bowled some poor spells before mopping up the tail. It wasn't a disaster by any means; it was six wickets in an Ashes Test match and I still have the ball at home as a keepsake. But I'd had dreams of taking an Ashes five-for, and they looked very different – more like Broad's 5 for 37 at The Oval in 2009. I think that's only natural: whenever you're aspiring to do something, you dream about the absolute best-case scenario that could play out. The trouble is that thinking like that when things are going well means that your negative feelings are compounded further if shit ever hits the fan.

Whenever someone in the team ticked off an individual achievement, someone else would stand up and acknowledge it in front of everyone in the dressing room. For my six-for, it was David Saker, our Australian bowling coach, at the end of a tough third day in the field. We were a long way behind in the game, trailing by more than 200 runs, and the mood was pretty sombre. Sakes didn't beat around the bush. He said, 'You didn't bowl that great today, but it was a good team effort and you're the one who got the rewards.' I thought, 'Oh fuck.' I was self-aware enough to know that I was super self-critical, but that moment reinforced the idea that what I'd been thinking was actually true: that I needed to be so much better in order to survive in this team.

The final two days of that Test were amazing to witness. I spent most of the fourth day in the dining room at the Gabba, only moving when we lost our first wicket. We didn't lose another in our second innings: Alastair Cook and Jonathan Trott put on an unbroken 329 before we finally declared on the final day at 517 for 1. We were all aware of Australia's brilliant record at the Gabba, which was their banker, and our top three were determined to rub their noses in the dirt to make a big statement at the start of the series. Strauss's declaration was designed to do the same; we were never going to bowl them out inside forty overs on a flat pitch, but we knew we could make life uncomfortable for them. Everything we did on that tour had a purpose: it was his way of showing that we were not there to fuck around, but to win.

In that final session, I hit Ricky Ponting on the head. If there was ever an opportunity to bomb someone with bouncers during Strauss's captaincy, he would throw me the ball. He wanted me to try to unsettle Australia. It felt like a statement: 'We are going to use our 21-year-old kid to bounce your captain, who is still one of the best players in the world – and it's going to work.' It was Strauss's way of saying that he wasn't just going to do things as they'd been done before. Broad got Katich out early, and when Ponting came in, it was bouncer time. The third ball I bowled to him was a sharp bouncer, which he ducked into; it pinged him on the helmet, skewed down to fine leg and he jogged through for a single.

I asked him if he was all right, and got nothing back from him. He just didn't acknowledge it. Jimmy and Swann had a go at me for it: 'What are you asking him that for?' But that was just my make-up, and much as I wondered if I was being weak by checking on him, I didn't ever regret doing it. After all, it was Ricky Ponting; I'd grown up loving watching him and his Australia team playing cricket, so of course I was going to ask if he was OK. We left the Gabba that night with the series still locked at 0–0, but felt almost like we'd won. Everyone was so positive about what we'd managed to do, especially given the position that we'd found ourselves in after three days. Previous England teams might have folded, but the fact that we didn't gave us confidence this tour would be different.

There was never much doubt that we'd win the Adelaide Test. Australia were panicking after the draw in Brisbane, making selection changes, and were 2 for 3 after choosing to bat on the first morning. I was at fine leg as Trott ran round from midwicket to run Katich out with a direct hit off the fourth ball of the match, and had the best view in the house: when he let go of the ball, I was looking over his right shoulder, and it was never doing anything other than hitting the stumps. Then Ponting and Clarke nicked off, and we were flying. There was a euphoric feeling throughout the team; a few players must have been carrying demons from Australia's comeback win there four years earlier, but you'd never have known it. Pietersen scored a brilliant double hundred; after his quiet summer, it was the first time I'd seen the real KP. I'd never witnessed anyone bat with that much bravado and sheer arrogance, taking the piss out of international bowlers. I'd watched him play like that on TV when I was younger, but seeing him first-hand highlighted just how confident he was. He walked across his stumps, hit boundaries on one leg – flamingo style – and smashed Xavier Doherty, their left-arm spinner, all over the place.

The only problem was that I didn't bowl quite as well as I knew I could, for the second Test in a row. I leaked runs on the first day, when everyone else had kept things tight. My only joy was when Marcus North feathered a back-of-a-length ball to Prior behind the stumps. In a different team, I might not have worried so much about my economy rate: I was a six-foot-eight fast bowler who could hit 90mph and had a knack of taking wickets. In 2010, there were three bowlers in the world with a strike rate below forty balls per wicket: Dale Steyn, Zaheer Khan and me. But to fit into that team under Flower and Strauss, you had to go at under three an over; if you didn't, you weren't bowling in the way that the team wanted. The watchword was 'control'. There was no acceptance of different individuals playing different roles. You either fitted into what the team demanded of you or you'd be dropped. I knew I had a great strike rate and a good average, but I was desperate to bring my economy rate down below three as well; if I did that, I'd be averaging 20 or 21, like Glenn McGrath did. If I achieved that, I'd be the best bowler in the world. It was an incredible amount of pressure to put on yourself as a young man.

The fourth day was hard graft. Broad went down with an abdominal strain, which meant we were playing with only three front-line bowlers. I held my own, nicked off Watson, and walked off that night with an economy rate of 2.9. *Got tighter to the stumps and bowled much better areas*, I wrote in my diary. *Economy under three an over for the first time all trip. Important I maintain that longer.* It was the one time on the trip that I felt as though I was fulfilling my role, and it felt amazing. I nicked off Watson with one that left him when he looked well set and bounced Mike Hussey out to crack the game open on the final morning, which proved to be a massive moment. The England supporters were going nuts underneath the scoreboard, and my favourite moment of the trip came when Swanny ripped a delivery through Peter Siddle's defences to take our sixth wicket of that final morning to wrap up our win before lunch. Whenever I visit Adelaide now, I still smile at the thought of it.

We went down into the dressing room to celebrate and, at the Adelaide Oval, the dressing rooms have no natural light. An hour after the close of play, someone went upstairs briefly and came back soaked; it was hacking it down with rain, and we'd been totally oblivious to it. If we'd taken any longer to get those last few wickets, the Aussies might have escaped with a draw. Instead, it was time to let our hair down; there was a decent gap before the Perth Test, with a warm-up in Melbourne that I knew I wasn't going to be playing in. We all went outside, and there was rain pouring down the tunnel to the dressing rooms. Paul Collingwood stripped down to his underpants, ran across the outfield and did a big Jürgen Klinsmann dive across the square. The celebrations were brilliant throughout that trip.

It was in Melbourne between the second and third Tests that I learned I'd been left out of the squad for the ODIs at the end of the tour. It wasn't a huge surprise because I'd hardly played any one-day cricket; after all, I'd been pulled out of domestic cricket for the ECB's strengthening programme that summer. But it still hurt and reinforced some of the negative thoughts I was having about my performances. *Gutted not to be in it*, I wrote. Even worse, I was told that I'd be heading over to the Caribbean to play for England Lions, who were due to take part in the West Indies domestic competition that winter. That confirmed it to me: what I was doing couldn't have been good enough. Being sent on that tour felt like I'd been told I didn't deserve the time off to decompress after the Ashes; I had to keep pushing forward to try and get better. I was naive at twenty-one, but I wasn't oblivious to the fact that touring Australia was the most intense thing I'd ever done in my life. I knew I would need some time to step back, which I wasn't going to get. *Going to be a massive comedown after the Ashes*, I added.

I probably dragged that disappointment into the third Test with me. We had a decent first day as a team, bowling Australia out for 268, but I took a pasting. Chris Tremlett replaced Broad and bowled beautifully with shape and bounce, while I went at more than five runs per over. I struggled to cope with the sense of failure.

**16 December 2010**

Really really disappointed today. Felt good going into the day, as though I could prove that I am a good bowler. But have let myself and everyone down. For the first time ever I have been embarrassed to be playing for England. Cramps in my second spell didn't help and I slipped in my first spell, but didn't put enough balls in the right area. Important that I scrap this from my memory and get ready to go in the second innings. Do some work tomorrow with Sakes and try the long spikes.

Hopefully we can show the resolve that they didn't and fight to get a lead of about 100. If we can keep them out there then we can really make them worry. They will be searching for things to happen. Draw a line under everything that happened today and start afresh tomorrow. I am still taking my Test wickets at 25. Not bad for a 21-year-old. Important to remember I am just 21!

I was trying so desperately to prove – to others, but also to myself – that I deserved my opportunity that I snatched at it. I stopped bowling with freedom. Every time I had the ball in my hand during that Test, I felt like I tensed up. To bowl well you need to be loose and free. I was the complete opposite, tense and tight. It was the first time I'd put so much pressure on myself in such a negative way. Trem bowled so well that I could feel my chance slipping away in the long term; I knew Broad would be back in when he was fit again, and with every bad ball I was dragging myself down the pecking order. There was enough pressure as it was: a massive game in an Ashes series, with a hostile crowd and an intense dressing room. Add in the pressure I put on myself and it snowballed into a horrible experience. I couldn't escape that sense that I didn't belong. It was only exacerbated by the fact that Mitchell Johnson bowled out of his skin. I was meant to be playing that same role for us, as a genuinely quick strike bowler, but I was all over the place and leaking runs.

The crowd were getting to me, too – at least, more accurately, one bloke in the members' stand. He'd been one of the only fans at the WACA nearly six weeks earlier for our first warm-up game, leaning over the boundary boards and spraying us for three days. He was on his own, drinking, and telling us how shit we were: 'It's going to be a long fuckin' summer, boys! You're going to get your fuckin' arses handed to you.' I thought it was pretty funny. We'd been around the country, gone 1–0 up, and now here he was again, in the very same seat. 'I remember you, Finn,' he'd tell me while I was fielding at fine leg. 'You were fuckin' shit during the tour game, and you're still fuckin' shit now.' I got Phil Hughes out on the second evening, caught in the slips, and finally bit: I turned around and gave the guy the big 'shush', with my finger on my lips. Deep down, though, I felt like he had a point: I took five expensive wickets in the match, but knew I was battling.

We lost the third Test heavily, and I didn't have a single positive feeling coming out of that week. As we travelled to Melbourne, I had a sinking feeling that, despite us winning eight of my eleven Test matches to date, my run in the England team was about to come to an end.

The Boxing Day Test at the MCG is one of sport's great occasions: a festive crowd, a vast stadium, a brilliant city and an annual tradition combining to create an incredible atmosphere. I had dreamed of playing in one, but it came down to me vs Tim Bresnan. As Strauss walked towards me in the cavernous away dressing room, my heart sank. 'Oh fuck,' I thought. 'This is actually happening.' Any decent captain knows not to drop a player in front of their teammates, so, as I was led away from the main part of the room, I knew it was over. We were tucked around the corner, standing in the bathroom area next to the hand dryers and the sinks, when he delivered the news that I knew was coming but still struggled to process.

## 25 December 2010

Worst Christmas Day ever. Was hopeful of retaining spot in team today. Felt good in practice. Strauss asked for two mins in the rooms and I knew I was fucked. 'Three things. 1. Fatigue. 2. Wicket. 3. Poor form. Two of these will be different in Sydney – make sure the third is.'

That is the most I've ever hurt. Playing for your country is amazing. Walking out on to the pitch is also amazing – national anthems, etc. Have done it for eleven Tests. Haven't been dropped since 2008. It hurts and hurts bad. Cried in the toilets and tried to keep it in in the announcement – but couldn't. Wished Bres good luck and I hope he does well. I'm just gutted and disappointed that I let this opportunity pass. With Tremlett bowling well and Broad coming back it could be curtains for me in international cricket for a while. Central contract, etc. gone. Will have to be twice the bowler I am to get anywhere now.

Forty-six wickets at 26 in eleven tests isn't good enough. Dinner with Lucy and family but didn't want to be anywhere. Just want to sit and think. As low as I have ever been.

Lucy was my girlfriend at the time, and had arrived just in time to see me dropped from the England team. So had my mum and my sister. I felt flat for myself, and sorry for them; they had hardly ever travelled, let alone long-haul, and it's not like our family had heaps of money. They'd come halfway across the world at significant cost to watch me play cricket for England in Australia, and at the first possible opportunity I'd failed to make their trip worthwhile. My parents weren't the type to put pressure on me, but I knew how proud they were of me up until that point. That was the hardest bit of it: the feeling I couldn't shake that I'd let them down. Happy

Christmas: I've got you tickets to every day of the Melbourne and Sydney Tests, not that I'm playing in either of them.

Strauss was a really good leader. He was very matter-of-fact when he spoke to you. He was direct and didn't bring emotion into decisions: both good traits for a captain. One of the tricky things about leadership roles in cricket – or any sport – is that you have to deal with a squad, not just a team. We had a sixteen-man squad, and he had to make sure that everyone was still pulling in the same direction as the series approached its climax. He would have known just how much it all meant to me; I'd played a lot with him, both for England and for Middlesex. He'd have remembered that net at Radlett when I was so desperate to impress him that I bowled at him for an hour on the day my grandad died. But he and Flower had to pick the team they thought would perform best in that Test match – and even though I was the leading wicket-taker in the series to that point, I wasn't in it.

As I sat on the team bus back to the hotel, I started to feel myself withdrawing from the rest of the squad. I was experiencing deep feelings of failure and rejection, which compounded into a realisation that I had messed things up for myself. It was only the second time in my career that I'd been dropped, and I'd taken it badly when it was just a couple of Division 2 games for Middlesex two years previously. Somehow, across six weeks in Australia, I'd gone from a sense of opportunity and an acceptance that things might not go perfectly to beating myself up after taking 14 wickets in three Ashes Tests because I'd conceded too many runs. It was very easy to be unpleasant to myself about it.

Being dropped was bad enough. Being dropped on Christmas Day was even worse. We had a team Christmas lunch in the hotel with all the partners and families, and it wasn't like I could go around telling people about it; as a squad, we had to keep things to ourselves until the toss the following morning, just in case anything happened in the interim. I felt so flat. It was weird enough being away from home for Christmas in the first place. The team management had organised a Father Christmas to come in and give gifts to players' kids, so I was sitting around watching them unwrap presents and trying to put on a brave face. It's funny the small details that stick in your memory about the highest and lowest points of your career. I can clearly remember the sound of the wife of one of our coaching staff tucking into some oysters. I hate the sound of people eating at the best of times, but those slurps were foul.

Boxing Day proved to be one of the most remarkable days of cricket I have ever witnessed. Australia managed 98 all out after Strauss put them in, and by the close we were 59 ahead without losing a wicket. I hated every second of it. It wasn't that I wasn't happy for my teammates, and naturally I wanted England to win. I just spent the day longing to be out there with my teammates. I was angry and disappointed with myself for throwing away the chance to be playing. For every day of England's Test cricket over the previous ten months, I'd been actively involved; now I was sitting in the dugout wearing a hi-vis vest and running on with the drinks. The worst moment was warming up before the toss, before the rest of the world knew that I'd been left out, and seeing the crowd start to filter into the stands. The pitch was a green-top, too, the type that makes bowlers salivate at the thought of bowling on, especially with the bounce in Australia making the nicks carry. Bres must have spent the first three Tests watching me from the sidelines thinking, 'I can bowl much better than this bloke,' and he proved it, taking six wickets in the match while hardly conceding a run. Competition for spots is what made us such a good attack; if I wasn't bowling well, Bres would have been, and if he wasn't, then Tremlett probably was. I just wished desperately that I could have been out in the middle rather than bowling overs at a stump during the lunch break.

I hated being twelfth man and didn't hide it well at all. I didn't want people to look at me and think I was happy to be dropped, or that I didn't care, because I thought it would make me an easy target in the future. There was a part of me that thought I should prove just how badly I was taking it, because it might play in my favour, so it wasn't a secret that I was absolutely gutted from my body language. But Huw Bevan, our strength and conditioning coach, pulled me aside and told me to stop moping about.

Bev was right: I was gutted that I wasn't out there, but I also wasn't the only person not playing. There were other guys nursing the frustration of not being picked: Eoin Morgan, Steve Davies, Ajmal Shahzad and Monty Panesar were all in the same boat as me. The difference was that they had all been left out throughout, whereas I was the only England player in the series to get dropped. It meant I felt the extra weight of rejection, inadequacy and failure, which I carried on my face throughout Boxing Day.

The fact that it was Bev who told me to pull myself together shows just how wrong I got it; he was a legend of a bloke, who has done well for himself since then in Welsh rugby. Australia's Phil Hughes, whom I'd played with at Middlesex, told me he couldn't believe I'd been dropped; maybe it was a bit of gamesmanship, or maybe just a guy the same age as me who had experienced being dropped himself in the 2009 Ashes. He'd come over before that series, and it was immediately clear that he was far too good for county cricket: he scored three hundreds in three games and was a great bloke to go with it.

It took us only ten sessions to win in Melbourne, and by lunchtime on the fourth day I was on the outfield doing the 'sprinkler' dance in front of the Barmy Army. It was a bizarre feeling, having not ridden the highs and lows to the same magnitude as the eleven guys playing, but I enjoyed that moment with the travelling fans a lot. It encapsulated how much fun we had as a squad across that trip. For all the stories I'd heard about how oppressive Australia could be, we managed to retain that sense of being a group of mates having a laugh on the other side of the world. Swanny spent the tour thinking he was Ricky Gervais, recording his video diary for the ECB's YouTube channel. It was just a massive piss-take, but helped the fans see a different side of us at a time when we didn't give much away to the press. We all played along with it and bought in, and it was the source of a lot of laughs.

It was that night that Cooky had to drag me out of my hotel room to celebrate – and I'm glad he did. We'd only retained the Ashes at that stage, but we were full of confidence that we'd seal the series in Sydney, and had enough of a gap between Tests that we could let ourselves go. Throughout the tour we had a really good relationship with the fans, and some of us would go and have a drink with the Barmy Army after most matches. It meant that the sense of camaraderie and us against them extended to the England supporters. As the tour went on, we sensed that the Australian public were turning on their team; at the end of the Melbourne Test, the only fans inside the MCG were English. If we walked into a bar at the start of the trip, the locals would tell us: 'You English are going to get nailed!' By the end, it was: 'We love how you guys are sticking it to the Aussies. Ponting is past it and we can't stand the rest of them.'

It was no surprise that I was left out again in Sydney.

Anderson, Tremlett and Bresnan had all bowled brilliantly at the MCG, and had plenty of time to recover. Our batters were unbelievable yet again. Cook, Bell and Prior all made hundreds, and we won by an innings for the third time in the series. Trem taking the wicket of Johnson produced some roar from the English fans, and they ruthlessly serenaded him to and from the crease. Lifting the urn itself felt a little hollow. You dream of being on the pitch for the winning moment, and it certainly doesn't feel the same when you're wearing a bib and sitting on the sidelines. I didn't feel present for most of that week – I was still trying to prove myself to the coaches while I was bowling in the middle during session breaks – but I was certainly there for the celebrations. As hard as I took being left out for those final two Tests, it was impossible not to get swept up by the sense of euphoria that surrounded our first Ashes win in Australia since 1986/87.

We spent a long time at the SCG after the final wicket fell, enjoying each other's company in the dressing rooms. Everyone was singing and dancing; Trotty sat himself down in an empty ice bath, and slid himself down a small set of stairs. Jimmy was curled up in a corner, exhausted emotionally, mentally and physically by the end of that series after playing all five Tests and taking 24 wickets. We went across to the Australian dressing room too; it's an old Ashes tradition that the two teams should share a drink together after the series. I caught up with Hughesy about what was next for both of us, and chatted with Steve Smith, who batted at number seven in that final Test match, as we had mutual friends from Sydney. I felt like Tom Cruise that night: we walked into a four-storey pub filled with England fans, and climbed all the way to the top past people celebrating and shouting our names. It was like nothing I'd ever experienced before in my life.

But the best bit had come straight after the game, out on the pitch, when we sat in a circle as a team and compared our favourite moments of the series. Mine was the last morning in Adelaide, when I'd taken the important wicket of Hussey and had experienced the winning moment in an Ashes Test match for the first time in my career. After the personal disappointment of the end of the series, that was what I clung on to; the memory of how good that crucial wicket had felt was one that I was desperate to taste again.

# 4

# Dead Ball

I arrived in Leeds in August 2012 knowing the scale of the challenge that I was about to face. Twelve months earlier, my England teammates had secured the number one spot in the ICC's Test rankings by thrashing India at home, but the 3–0 defeat to Pakistan that followed wiped away any sense of invincibility. We were up against an unbelievably strong South Africa side filled with all-time greats: Graeme Smith, Hashim Amla, Jacques Kallis, AB de Villiers, Dale Steyn and Morne Morkel. Man for man, they were the best cricket team I ever played against. De Villiers kept wicket from number 5, which meant they had proper batters down to number 7 as well as four top-class bowlers; in Kallis, they had – in my opinion – the greatest cricketer of all time. We were 1–0 down in the series, and needed to bounce back in the second Test at Headingley.

My worst fears at the end of the 2010/11 Ashes had come to pass: Tim Bresnan and Chris Tremlett were both ahead of me in the pecking order, and in the eighteen months after that series, I'd only played three Test matches. But I felt like I had become a much better bowler in that time: I'd been a regular in the one-day team, opening the bowling with good success against India, Pakistan and Australia. I'd climbed to number

3 in the ICC's bowling rankings in ODIs; now, my challenge was to replicate that form in Test cricket, which is where the best players rise to the very top.

Much as I hated the feeling of being overlooked, there were worse Test matches to miss than the first one of this South Africa series: Hashim Amla hit an unbeaten triple hundred on an absolute road at The Oval as South Africa racked up 637 for 2 declared, and we went down by an innings. Our seamers – Jimmy Anderson, Stuart Broad and Bresnan – had bowled a lot of overs for no reward, so I knew I would have a good chance to play at Headingley. Little did I know it would be alongside the three of them in an all-seam attack, with Graeme Swann left out. He was spewing about it, but his absence created a huge opportunity for me against a fantastic cricket team.

I'd been gutted to miss out on the India series the previous summer. When the guys were presented with the mace to mark the number 1 ranking, I had turned down an invitation to go to The Oval and celebrate with them because I didn't feel like I'd been part of it. An email went around to everyone who had been part of the squad asking us if we'd like to come down, but I'd been playing a 40-over game for Middlesex the day before and didn't think I should be there: I'd even been left out of the squad altogether for the first Test. It was a similar feeling to when we retained the Ashes in Melbourne: I didn't really consider myself part of that achievement, be-cause I'd only played one Test that whole summer and was so determined to get back in. I wasn't sulking, simply think-ing, 'Right, what do I need to do to get myself back into the side?' Of course, I'd played a proper role: I'd played in twelve of England's last twenty Tests, and we'd won eight of those games. But if you look back at the team photos of us lifting the mace, I am nowhere to be seen. In retrospect, I wish I had gone along and been part of those celebrations.

By then, I was really kicking on as a 50-over bowler and was opening the bowling for our ODI side. When we went to India at the start of the 2011/12 winter, Broad was injured and Anderson was rested. Suddenly, I was leading the attack. It was a brutal series: India had won the World Cup six months previously and were an unbelievable side. They beat us 5–0, though we did at least nick the T20 international that rounded out the tour. But it felt like a big moment for me: I had a real purpose in that side, and loved the responsibility of it. Andy Flower even singled me out for praise.

Like any sportsman, I really hated losing, and getting thrashed like that meant I was fired up at a few points in that series. It was my first experience of playing in front of huge crowds in India, and witnessing the crazy, unrivalled level of passion for the game that their fans have: people love cricket in Australia and England, but it's not that wild atmosphere of fans screaming and the sound bouncing off the roof of the stadium. In Mumbai, I got myself in trouble: I gave Suresh Raina a massive send-off, and Virat Kohli wasn't happy about it. There's a great photo of me towering over Kohli and MS Dhoni, with Jonathan Trott trying to pull me away from them as though we're having a scrap outside a bar. I was bowling quick – up at 93mph/150kph – without really trying to, which was a sign of being in great rhythm, and I felt like I had bowled well enough to be part of a winning team, even though we lost every game. We all ended up in the match referee's room to get a ticking off: Dhoni, Kohli and Raina on one side, with me and Alastair Cook on the other. 'This is a bad image for the game,' we were told, while we looked at our feet; I'd played a fair bit against Kohli at Under-19s level, and knew that if

I caught his eye then neither of us would be able to avoid bursting out laughing.

I'd always seen intimidation as an important element of fast bowling: you can't be a great fast bowler without having some kind of presence about you. If you are seen as being meek, and someone who turns away from battles and challenges, then that doesn't send the right message – either to the opposition, or to your own teammates. I'm not a confrontational person off the field, but I loved the feeling of going into combat. Later in my career, I was expending too much energy on my own internal battles and not enough time on the battle at the other end of the pitch, but in my early twenties, I was so confident that I could really let it rip. When I was growing up, I loved putting in a big tackle in a game of football, or nudging people around on the basketball court. (And yes, to answer the question I have been asked more than any other as a six feet eight inch athlete, I did play a bit of basketball.) Maybe I took it a bit too far that night with the send-off of Raina, but I showed India that I had an edge to me.

From India, I flew over to New Zealand. I had a rare gap in my schedule and there was no competitive cricket to play back home during the English winter, so I had organised a deal to play domestically for Otago. If I'd been playing a decade later, I'd probably have been looking to earn some money in T20 cricket during that window, during one of the many franchise leagues; instead, I was playing first-class cricket without being paid a penny. All they covered was my accommodation and rented me a car, but the truth was that I wasn't fussed about the financial aspect: I wanted to experience bowling with a Kookaburra ball in first-class cricket, after struggling with it at times during the Ashes the previous winter, and it was a great opportunity to become a bit more self-sufficient. I'd always travelled as part of a team, so this was the first time that I was left to my own devices overseas, and I saw it as a reconnaissance mission before England's tour to New Zealand the following winter. I lived in Dunedin, and my teammates took me under their wing: Jimmy Neesham and Hamish Rutherford were there, along with Brendon and Nathan McCullum. I opened the bowling with Neil Wagner, and finished the trip feeling like I was ready to go back and make the most of my next opportunity in Test cricket.

I was particularly disappointed not to play in the Test series against Pakistan in the UAE at the start of 2012. I felt like I had made such big strides in my game since losing my place during the Ashes, and was bowling as fast as I ever had before. I was miffed to miss out on selection, and had to sit and watch as we got spun out by Saeed Ajmal and Abdur Rehman – though I'm not sure I'd have contributed much with the bat against those two. When it came to the one-dayers, I had the added motivation of wanting to show Flower that he should have picked me in the Tests. I bowled as well as I ever had, and took 13 wickets in our 4–0 series whitewash: my speeds were consistently above 90mph/145kph, and my economy rate was down below 3.5 runs per over. I felt like I was becoming the complete package, and getting closer and closer to being the bowler that I had spent the last two years chasing.

I finally got my place in the Test team back in Sri Lanka, helping us to secure a 1–1 draw with a hard-fought win in Colombo. It was tough graft: it must have been 45 degrees centigrade, and a day in the field left you feeling as though you needed to be put on a drip. Monty Panesar was twelfth man and fell into a post-lunch stupor with his sunglasses over his eyes. We were gasping for a drink on the pitch, and nobody could get his attention; Flower had to come sprinting down from the dressing room to wake him up, and – quite rightly – let him know what for. I bowled 37.5 overs on a surface that didn't really suit me, but our plan was all about bowling dry and letting Swann attack from the other end. I went at 2.14 runs per over across both innings, my best-ever economy rate in a Test match, and came away feeling like I'd acquitted myself as well as I could have hoped.

The trouble was, we were such a strong side that by the time the home season started against the West Indies in May 2012, I was running the drinks again. Tim Bresnan got the nod ahead of me for the first two Tests of that series, and was man of the match at Trent Bridge. People forget just how good Bresnan was: it was no coincidence that England won every single one of the first thirteen Tests that he played in. It was such a strong era of England fast bowlers, and I consider myself very lucky to have played in it: Anderson and Broad were on their way to becoming all-time greats, and I was generally competing with Bresnan and Tremlett for the third spot while Graham Onions, Liam Plunkett and Ajmal Shahzad waited in the wings. If I'd been around at a different time, maybe I would have won more caps and had longer runs in the side, but it meant I never took anything for granted. It never felt like I was just being given a game for the sake of it, or because it was the default: I knew that if I wanted to play for that England team, then I had to earn every single cap.

Before we played South Africa, I had the chance to face Australia for the first time since the 2010/11 Ashes tour. Mercifully, I never ended up going on the England Lions tour that I'd been dreading; we had a couple of injuries, so I was kept on for the ODIs that followed those Tests. But this was my chance to prove myself against them, and to show them that I had improved from eighteen months previously. I went into that series knowing I meant business, and proved it with eight wickets in four matches as we won 4–0. We were on a winning streak in ODIs, but the truth is that it mainly felt like a building block or a stepping stone towards Test cricket; rightly or wrongly, that was the English attitude towards white-ball cricket at the time. I was troubling their best players, and David Warner – my old Middlesex teammate – said that I would be a handful to face in the back-to-back Ashes series that were looming in 2013 and 2013/14.

My best performance in that series came at Chester-le-Street. I took four wickets – two separate sets of two in two balls – and continued to feel like everything had clicked. I was chuffed to get Michael Clarke out, who had taken over from Ricky Ponting as Australia captain, and the ball that dismissed him summed up everything I was about: running in hard, getting very tight to the stumps on release, and hitting a good length at decent pace and nipping it off the seam to knock back his off stump. In fact, I was so tight to the stumps on release that I knocked the bails with my knee in my delivery stride: Michael Atherton briefly mentioned it on TV commentary, but Clarke made no mention. I'm a tall man with long limbs, and had often struggled to keep total control over my body while releasing the ball: early in my career, I would regularly lose my footing and tumble over. But in my mind, it was well established that some bowlers would knock the bails off when they bowled – although usually with their hand, rather than their knee. My idol, Glenn McGrath, did it often as a result of how tight he used to get to the stumps; so did Shaun Pollock, the great South African seamer.

But fast-forward to that first morning at Headingley for the second Test against South Africa, and that quirk became a serious problem. I arrived at the ground that day raring to go, and ready for a crack at a formidable, in-form South African top order. I felt like I was back, and had prepared better than ever with my planning. We knew Graeme Smith, their captain and opening batter, was an unusual player in that he scored almost all of his runs through the leg side, so we left a huge gap between straight mid-off and backward point and said, 'If you want to try and hit one through there, be my guest.' In my second over, he fell right into the trap: I angled one across him, which he nicked straight to Strauss at first slip, and for a split second, I thought I had marked my return to the team in perfect fashion.

But before I could celebrate, I heard Steve Davis saying, 'Dead ball.' I turned around, and he gestured to the stumps at the non-striker's end; I had knocked the bails off with my knee. 'You'll put the batsman off if you kick the stumps,' he said, as Strauss and Bresnan came over to ask what had happened. I stood there with my hands on my hips, completely bemused. I wasn't angry, just baffled: I'd never even heard of that being a dead ball. I'd done it through the summer without a problem – I'd even done it twice in my first over that morning – and ever since I could remember, I'd seen it happen without any negative consequences. I almost felt cheated: it felt to me like someone had just invented this thing on the spot.

It turned out that Smith and Alviro Petersen, his opening partner, had been in the ears of the umpires, complaining that they'd been distracted by me dislodging the bails. It never made any sense to me: my release point was nowhere near the stumps, so why would you be looking at them? If you're looking at the stumps while I'm releasing the ball, you probably shouldn't be an international opening batter. The most ridiculous bit was that it set a precedent: Smith hit me for two fours later that day, and both of them were called dead balls, so he didn't get the runs for them. I thought, 'It can't have been that fucking distracting, if he can still hit me for four.'

The problem stemmed from my running style. I was a decent runner growing up – I did athletics at school, where the 200 metres was my race – but for some reason, when I put a cricket ball in my hand, I'd run slightly differently: my feet crossed over a little bit in my natural gait. As I got to the crease, I'd slow down a little bit – which felt natural to me – and that would exacerbate the crossing over of my feet. My last step with my right foot would be quite a big step across, so to rebalance myself, I'd have to jump back in order to get close to the stumps. It sounds incredibly technical, and I only know this after watching slowed-down footage in close detail to try and work out what was happening; in my head, I was just running in normally.

I hate making excuses, but it clearly affected me that week. I'd built it up as the first time for nearly two years that I'd really warranted selection in a home Test. I wasn't picked by default, because someone else was injured or rested; I was bowling well, and we were playing what we thought were our best four bowlers for those conditions. All that went through my mind was, 'This is ridiculous.' I tried not to let it overwhelm my thoughts, but I didn't know what would come next: would knocking the bails off always be a dead ball now? Or would there be a reset at the end of the match? It was a strange, rain-affected Test match, but my figures weren't great and I felt like the whole thing had thrown me off course.

I was so annoyed with Steve Davis, who I felt had buckled under pressure from Smith. Bizarrely, it was over a decade later that I discovered Rod Tucker – who was standing at square leg – had instigated it. We were both working at the 2024 T20

World Cup – me for the BBC, and him as an umpire – and had a few beers together one night. It somehow came up in conversation – probably from me sounding off about the decision – and he said, 'Aw, mate, you do realise it was me who did you over there?' I couldn't believe it! They'd been chatting to each other at the end of the over or via their walkie-talkies, and Tucker had told Davis, 'You have to call dead ball.' I told Rod that I was over it, but I'm still not sure that I am.

Everything about what happened felt wrong to me. It was being discussed as though nobody had ever knocked the bails off when they were bowling before, which I knew wasn't true. Whenever I bowled at my best, my energy was fully focused on the battle with the batsman at the other end; my run-up would feel natural, and my thoughts would be trained on the tactical aspects of bowling. The dead-ball call suddenly brought my attention to my run-up itself. It planted a seed of doubt at the top of my mark, distracting me from what I was doing with the ball and dragging my focus towards the angle of my run-up and my rhythm as I ran in, knowing that any deceleration would prompt my right knee to jut out and dislodge the bails. It took some time for that seed to germinate but once it did, it was hard to focus on anything else.

My own issues had been overshadowed by the time we left Leeds. Kevin Pietersen hit an outrageous second-innings 149, smacking Steyn all over Headingley; it was an absolute joke of a hundred, and enough to capture plenty of attention on its own. But on the final evening, he then walked into a press conference and started shooting from the hip: 'It's tough being me in this dressing room and playing for England.' We were crowded around a tiny TV in the dressing room, saying, 'Has he really just said that?' When we arrived at Lord's, KP had been dropped after it emerged that he had been texting

South Africa players about Strauss. There were team meetings about what had happened, but as I saw it, there was just a total breakdown of trust. Kev was also aggrieved about the 'KP Genius' Twitter account, a parody at his expense which he was convinced some players were involved in. It led to the whole thing blowing up. I was still a junior within the dressing room, so it wouldn't have crossed my mind to get involved at all in those meetings: my sole focus was on trying to prove myself on my home ground after my personal disappointment the week before.

I kept my place ahead of Bresnan, and playing at Lord's helped me put kneeing the stumps out of my mind. Bowling from the Pavilion End, I knew I could afford to go that fraction wider on the crease because the slope would help me to angle the ball back in naturally. I was gutted to lose the Test and see the South Africans dancing around with the mace, but I knew that I had bowled as well as I could. I walked off after our second innings feeling like I was back for good in an England shirt. Finally, I had translated two summers and one winter of consistent performance in county cricket and ODIs into a Test match. I took four wickets in both innings and, in the second, I bowled the best spell of my career.

Scores were almost level after both teams' first innings, and South Africa were 249 for 4 in their second when I was thrown a six-over-old second new ball. I bowled more than 10,000 deliveries in international cricket, but I remember that spell as clearly as any other. My run-up was punchy: it felt like my feet were barely hitting the floor, and I had to use very little energy as I accelerated towards the crease. I'd hold my top speed in my approach, jump, and then time paused: I was at the top of my action, with my eyes level and my body coiled, ready to release. Then came the sense of snap and zip off the end of my fingertips. This was how I bowled at my very best, and particularly from the Pavilion End at Lord's: I'd played there so much for Middlesex that I used it to my advantage. I bowled with a slightly scrambled seam to the right-handers, threatening both edges of the bat by hitting a hard length – forcing them to play – and angling it in towards off stump, confident that it would nip one way or the other.

In the first innings, I'd got Amla with a ball that nipped back in; this time, I pitched the ball in the same spot and it seamed away past his outside edge, kissing the top of his off stump. He'd made yet another hundred by that point, but I had given us an opening. In my next over, it was that same length again that accounted for de Villiers: the ball nipped away off the seam to take his outside edge, and skewed straight to Strauss at first slip. Then came two overs from around the wicket to the left-handers, JP Duminy and Jacques Rudolph: my angle on the crease brought the ball into them, but the slope would take it away from their outside edge. Duminy escaped, but I squared Rudolph up with one that moved away just a fraction off the seam; he edged it through to Matt Prior, and I felt as though I had changed the momentum of the game with three quick wickets. I walked off thinking, 'I'm back. I'm a proper Test bowler here.'

Late on the first day, I'd made a big mistake: with the light fading, I bowled a short ball which smacked Steyn on the chest. I realised straight away how stupid I'd been: Steyn was arguably the best bowler in the world, and one of the quickest, and would be sure to give as good as he got. That evening, I bumped into him when I was coming back from the close of play press conference. I asked him if he was OK: he was my favourite opposition bowler to watch of the modern era after all. He replied in the most matter-of-fact way possible, telling me he was fine in a tone of voice that made clear to me he wasn't going to forget what I'd done. Two days later, it was my turn in the firing line: he peppered me with short balls, one of which smacked me on the helmet. I did get one away though, nailing a pull through square leg; I can still picture the ball racing away to the boundary in front of the Mound Stand.

It's not always the case at international level, but in domestic cricket, there can be a bit of a bowlers' union: you only bounce fellow fast bowlers as a last resort. I remember vividly a game against Sussex in 2018, when a young Jofra Archer was making a nuisance of himself with the bat in hand. Dawid Malan, my Middlesex captain, instructed me to bowl him a bouncer from mid off. 'Really?' I thought. I'd seen clips of Jofra bowling and I wasn't sure I wanted to piss him off. But you do as your captain says and I bowled him a decent bouncer. Boing. It clonked him on the helmet. He passed his concussion checks and continued batting but the following morning I saw him in the Long Room as we walked out to go and warm up. 'How are you, Jofra?' I asked him. His only response was, 'You'll be getting that back, Steve.' I spent the next 24 hours shitting my pants. Then, inevitably, it was Jofra bowling when I walked out to bat. Would he follow the fast bowlers' union rule of only bouncing a bowler out of desperation? My eyes were trained looking for a yorker. But before I knew it, the ball was in front of my face and squeezing my right index finger against the bat handle. I took five minutes to compose myself after a visit from the physio, and I spooned the next ball straight to square leg from in front of my face again. I've never been so happy to be out in my life. That finger is still swollen to this day.

South Africa's win at Lord's brought the Test summer to an end, and Strauss – whose 100th Test had been overshadowed by the KP saga – stepped down as captain a few days later, retiring from all formats of cricket. He wrote each of us a short letter to let us know just before he made his decision public, which were delivered to us in the dressing rooms at the Rose Bowl during the subsequent ODI series. In mine, he reflected he could have picked me more often than he did: since my initial run of eleven consecutive caps in 2010, I had only played five of England's next twenty Tests, and was heartened to learn that Strauss agreed that it could easily have been far more. It was the sort of personal touch that I really appreciated, and I cherished that note for some time.

The intensity of our England schedule back then was hard to fathom: players often speak out about how draining the international calendar is in the modern era, but I knew nothing different. We were constantly on the road: the home season ended with those white-ball fixtures against South Africa, leading into a World T20, which led into a Test series against India; after Christmas, we went back there for a white-ball series, then straight on to New Zealand for more white-ball games and into a Test series. It was like running on a treadmill turned up to a high speed: it felt great while you were on it, but there was never much chance of keeping pace for a sustained period of time.

At the World T20, my issues with kneeing the stumps returned. When we played New Zealand in Pallekele, James Franklin drove me through mid-off for four – but because I'd knocked the bails off, the umpire called dead ball. It summed up how ridiculous the situation was: clearly, I'd rather not have been doing it, but Smith claiming he'd been put off was just an excuse for edging me to slip. Franklin was livid that he had missed out on a perfectly legitimate boundary, and even more so when my follow-up delivery nipped back and hit him in the groin.

We missed out on the semi-finals, but I felt in great rhythm throughout that tournament: I bowled a quick spell at Chris Gayle against the West Indies, and took 3 for 16 in that win against New Zealand. It felt like I was heading towards our tour of India in good form and, after my previous success there in one-day cricket, I was desperate to keep proving myself at Test level. But if knocking the bails off was one problem to contend with, then the knock-on effects of my attempts to solve it would become another altogether.

# 5

# Backed into a Corner

Any international fast bowler will tell you that their run-up is a key component of their bowling, because it is the source of their natural flow. Morne Morkel's pirouette, Pat Cummins's loop around, Josh Hazlewood's distinctive angle and Jasprit Bumrah's stutters should prove that there is no right or wrong way to approach the crease: all that matters is that you are gathering momentum as you run in, and finding the rhythm and flow that feels natural to you.

I was always a rhythm bowler. I needed that sense of rhythm and fluency to feel confident about how I was bowling, which is why I bowled a lot more than some others in training. I was very methodical with the way I went about the motion of bowling. I saw it as a lap of a circuit. Before my first over in a match, I'd pick out a couple of advertising boards that I would make sure I read to myself before each ball I bowled; the act of reading the companies' names would clean the slate from the ball before and change my focus to the next ball. In the second half of 2012, when I was bowling as well as I ever had done before, my mind would be totally clear.

I'd make sure that my fingers were dry and that the ball was in my hand as I wanted, and then take off. I would punch off the balls of my feet at the beginning of my run-up, and since I was a decent runner at school, I would get up to speed quickly. I'd have twelve strides at full pace, pumping my knees, and would hit a cruising speed halfway through my run-up. As soon as I got to my jump, there would be a pause. It felt as though time stood still for a split second as I leapt up. My eyes were level, focusing on the top of the batter's off stump. I would let my levers unfold, standing as tall as possible and unloading everything towards the batter over a fully braced front leg. When I released the ball, I felt a sting off the end of my fingertips as the hard seam of the ball left my hand. It was only a tiny snap, but it was the one that I found the most satisfying: if I was struggling for rhythm, that was the feeling that I craved more than any other.

My run-up was always relatively long: David Saker, the England bowling coach, used to tell me that I could bowl at the same pace off a much shorter run-up. He said that I'd conserve more energy, which would allow me to maintain my pace for longer. I was so headstrong and confident as a young player that I never listened to him. My attitude was that people could offer me advice all they wanted, but, ultimately, this was my career, not theirs. I took responsibility for it. One of the advantages I saw in the length of my run-up was that it gave me time to digest what was going on in an over: I had a routine that I stuck to, and fell back on it if I was hit for four or had a catch dropped off my bowling. I had a couple of small technical pointers that I focused on: tucking my elbow in, keeping my front arm close to my hip, and making sure my follow-through was on the cut strip so that all my energy was going towards the batter. But when I was bowling well, all of those things became second nature. I could just focus on where I wanted to bowl the ball, and how I was going to get the guy at the other end out.

The dead-ball issue that had developed at Leeds threatened to throw all of that off, but I found a way to overcome it on our tour to India. I used the white bowling markers that most bowlers would place at the top of their marks, and put them on the ground right up near the umpire. The idea was that if my right foot landed on the left-hand side of the marker, it was impossible for me to jump in enough to hit the stumps: I just physically couldn't jump that far to the right at the pace that I was running. I paced it out with my feet, put the marker down, and resolved that I would just have to ignore any funny looks from the umpires: this was what I felt I had to do to avoid the problem, and it worked.

But my series was nearly over before it started. On the first morning of our first warm-up match in India, I was fielding at mid-on when an India A batter worked the ball away towards midwicket. No sooner had I started sprinting after it, I felt a sharp pain in my right thigh; as it turned out, I'd managed to strain my quadriceps muscle. I tried to jog back to my fielding position, but I knew immediately that I was in trouble. I had to leave the field before bowling the second over of my spell, and a scan the next day confirmed the problem: it was a small tear, but enough to rule me out of the first Test at the very least.

I was frustrated, but mainly upset: I had jumped ahead of Tim Bresnan at the end of the summer, and knew I was in line to start the series. We'd stopped off in Dubai on the way to India for fitness testing, and were back on the plane the next day; soon after, we were at the Cricket Club of India in Mumbai for the warm-up match. Injuries can happen whenever, but I'm sure the combination of long-haul flights and pushing myself hard for fitness tests can't have helped. I was always a bad traveller: I struggled really badly to overcome jet lag, and it used to take me a bit longer than everyone else to get up to speed with being in a new country. The timing was cruel: I'd missed out on all those Test matches over the previous two years, then had come into the tour feeling as fit as I'd ever been and bowling at good pace only to hurt myself in the very first session. I'd always had niggles throughout my career, but this was my first real experience of a proper injury that would rule me out of playing for England.

I assumed that I'd be flying home, but Andy Flower said: 'No, we want you here. We need you. If you can play one Test, you'll play one Test.' That was a huge boost to my confidence, and confirmed that I was doing something right. It meant a long few weeks of rehab, being as diligent as I possibly could to try and get myself in the right shape to play a part in the series.

We came into the series determined after the home defeat to South Africa, and while India's batting line-up might appear strong on paper years later – Virender Sehwag, Gautam Gambhir, Cheteshwar Pujara, Sachin Tendulkar, Virat Kohli, Yuvraj Singh and MS Dhoni – we didn't look at it with any fear. We'd beaten them 4–0 at home in the 2011 summer, and while we knew they'd be strong in their own conditions, they didn't have a scary attack; there was no sense that we were in for a pounding, like most England teams that have been over there since. It felt like a fresh start, with Kevin Pietersen being 'reintegrated' into the side and Alastair Cook taking over from Andrew Strauss as captain. We sat in a hotel meeting room in Mumbai and heard KP, Cooky and Flower say their piece: 'Let's pull together here and create something special.' If there was any animosity still there towards KP from our senior players, I didn't realise it: I was so wrapped up in my own hunt to be on the team sheet at the start of the series that I never worried too much about those other dynamics within the dressing room.

We had a new face in our squad on that trip who I had been

told was a good young player, but hadn't seen much up close and seemed like a left-field pick. But it only took me one nets session to realise that Joe Root was a serious talent, even at the age of twenty-one. At the end of the first Test in Ahmedabad – which we lost – I was building back up towards a decent level of intensity, and picked up a reverse-swinging ball because I fancied a bit of a confidence boost. I had a clear method with reverse swing: away, away, away, away, and then set them up for the big inswinger, ideally to knock off stump out of the ground. He watched every ball intently, and I didn't get him out once: he would leave the away-swinger, play the inswinger through mid-on, duck under the bouncer and then go back to leaving the away-swinger. I thought, 'This has done for good international batsmen before. What's going on?' I won't pretend that I knew he would go on to become England's highest-ever run scorer, but I realised immediately that he was a real star. Even at that age, he seemed so comfortable in that dressing room environment: he was a cheeky chappy, mucking around and playing pranks on the players whom he'd grown up watching on TV.

It was during the Test series that I decided to enter the auction for the Indian Premier League for the first time. I'd had a good year in white-ball cricket: I was leading our ODI attack and hadn't been hit for a single six at the T20 World Cup. If not now, when? I knew playing in India would mean missing the start of the county season, but I didn't feel like I had to prove that I was good enough to play for England by bowling hundreds of overs for Middlesex: I'd already shown it. I knew it would be a long winter, but I didn't know any difference from being on the road. I got all the forms sorted with my agent, Rich Hudson, and sat in the business centre of a hotel signing documents with a real sense of excitement that I might be on the cusp of an amazing experience – and a decent payday.

But the ECB had other ideas. I was on an England contract, so the ECB were my employer, and I needed their blessing – via a No-Objection Certificate – to go and play in India. I was summoned by Flower at the hotel, and John Carr, their director of operations, sent me an email saying: 'Just a brief note to confirm that I will not now be submitting your IPL auction agreement.' As chance would have it, I was sitting in a hotel room with Kevin and Eoin Morgan, who had both told me how brilliant the IPL was, just before my meeting with Andy. Kev told me, 'It doesn't matter what Flower says: you tell him you're putting your fucking name into that auction.' He was a massive advocate for the IPL. It was an easy sell: the tournament's great, you're chatting to the best players in the world all the time, and you're well paid for it. It was a no-brainer.

The establishment didn't see it like that. They were much more old-school in their thinking: the feeling was that playing in the IPL was almost like turning your back on English cricket. The global landscape was so different: I grew up in the era where your only way to make good money playing cricket was by playing Tests and earning a central contract, not by flying around the world and dipping in and out of T20 leagues. Flower's attitude was simple: 'We need you to play in the Championship at the start of the summer,' he told me. They wanted to control how much I was bowling, and he wasn't offering me any guarantees over my spot. I was disappointed, but my focus was on playing as many Tests as I could for England so I held no animosity. It was annoying, but I assumed the opportunity to go over to the IPL would come up again; as things panned out, that was the closest I ever got.

I was fit and fresh for the third Test at Eden Gardens in Kolkata. I'd worked so hard in my rehab to ensure I could play a part in the series, which we levelled in Mumbai thanks to another incredible KP innings. I played a tour match for the Lions over in Navi Mumbai to prove my fitness and showed I was ready to go: I took four wickets on the first day, then watched Root open the batting and hit 166. I'd spent my first couple of years in international cricket knowing that James Anderson and Stuart Broad were – quite rightly – ahead of me in the pecking order, but I was so confident and hungry by this stage that I felt like I was creeping up behind them. That was more or less confirmed by Flower's decision in Kolkata: Broady had been struggling with a niggle and hadn't made as much of an impact in the series as he'd have liked, so I replaced him as one of two seamers alongside Jimmy. For the first time, I was considered the second-best available seamer in the country.

Ten overs into the Test match, I found myself in the same position that I'd been in five weeks earlier: chasing a ball towards the midwicket boundary, running back from mid-on. But this time, Samit Patel was racing after it too, and put in a big dive to cut it off; I hurled the ball in towards Matt Prior, and inexplicably, Sehwag was stranded halfway down the pitch after a mix-up with Gautam Gambhir. It was a gift of a wicket, and got us off to a great start. Anderson, who bowled unbelievably on that tour, got both Kohli and Tendulkar, and I got on the board with a sharp short ball to Dhoni on the second morning. It was one of my favourite Test wickets: he had always got the better of me in one-dayers, and was fast becoming the biggest name in Indian cricket, but my extra pace and bounce were too much for him. We took a huge lead, thanks to Cook's 190, and in the second innings, I bowled as well as I ever had outside of England: my figures were 3 for

45 from 21 overs, my pace was consistently in the high 80s, and I had the ball reversing to get Kohli and Zaheer Khan out.

I had a back spasm on the final morning, which was a frustrating setback: Bresnan came back in for the decider in Nagpur, a real grind of a draw which helped us clinch the series 2–1 after our win in Kolkata. By then, Broady and I had flown home: we joked that we were like two injured soldiers on the plane, with my back giving up and him struggling with a fat-pad issue in his foot. With hindsight, I wish I'd stayed for the celebrations, but after a long tour and with a non-stop schedule, a few extra days at home before Christmas felt utterly priceless. What's more, I actually felt fully part of the win this time: it was an amazing achievement, England's first series win in India since 1984/85, and although I'd only played one Test, I'd more than held my own and felt like I would have played them all if my body had allowed. My form was good enough that whenever I was fit, I was playing, and was an important part of our attack across all three formats.

In the short term, I knew we had a big series in New Zealand coming up and felt well prepared for the challenge we'd face over there, having had a taste of conditions during my stint at Otago. But there was something bigger on the horizon, something that meant that much more to us as England players: back-to-back Ashes series, culminating in the 2013/14 tour to Australia. As every cricket fan knows, the Ashes are held twice within a four-year cycle: once in England and once in Australia, with enough of a gap between each series for a fresh narrative to build. But with the 2015 Cricket World Cup in mind, the ECB and Cricket Australia decided that they had to change the cycle. In theory, it made sense, since England would so often arrive at a World Cup underprepared and exhausted after a long, hard tour to Australia. Their solution, though, was just to cram as much cricket in as possible: we would play the 2013 Ashes at home, then head Down Under a couple of months later. It meant ten Ashes Tests in the space of six months, and it's not like it solved the problem long term: in 2019, England staged the Ashes immediately after a World Cup on home soil.

But at twenty-three and bowling as well as I ever had in an England shirt, I wasn't too bothered by the details of the scheduling. All I saw was the opportunity to prove to everyone – and to the Australians in particular – just how far I had come since the 2010/11 series. I was determined that we would dominate them at home and then make it four Ashes wins in a row in Australia, and I was bullish that I would be a huge part of England's success.

The trouble was, my bowling-marker solution to my run-up problem wasn't foolproof. We were back in India for the one-day leg of our tour in early 2013, and were much more competitive than we had been on our last visit, losing 3–2 rather than 5–0. But in Mohali, I had a second wicket chalked off for kneeing the stumps in my action – by Steve Davis again, no less – and it proved costly. It was a similar delivery and dismissal: I was trying to push the ball across a left-hander – Suresh Raina this time, rather than Graeme Smith – and again had him caught at first slip, but Davis waved his arms to signal dead ball. Cooky made it clear that he disagreed with the decision, but I'd been deemed a 'serial offender' after doing it a couple of times at the start of the series.

The thing is, I bowled nearly 50 overs in that one-day series, and hit the stumps with my knee two or three times. It's not like I was doing it every ball, by any means. But that seed of doubt had started to sprout; there were murmurs about technical changes, and what I could do differently in my run-up to solve my issues. The MCC were also making noises about potential changes to the Laws of Cricket, which was unsettling. Clearly, something needed to change: the dead-ball situation had become farcical. I knew that things couldn't carry on like this forever.

I'd always managed to push back against Saker's suggestion that I should try shortening my run-up, but I felt like I had gradually been backed into a corner over the previous six months. In the second T20I we played against New Zealand, in Hamilton, I bowled OK but had a nagging sense of distraction: I was very conscious of what I was doing with my body in my action, and saw that my speeds were down on where they'd been earlier in the winter. I felt like something had to change, but I needed a quick fix: the schedule was so incessant that I wouldn't have time to take myself away and spend weeks working on my running style to solve the problem at its root. I was so desperate to secure my status as a three-format regular that missing games never even crossed my mind as an option.

The day before the second ODI in Napier, I relented. I would often bowl off a shorter run-up in the nets anyway, since my full one was pretty long. But this felt nice. I ran in hard to try and replicate match intensity from the shorter run-up and the ball was zipping through. It was the result of some encouragement from others, sure, but this was very much my decision. I wish it hadn't, but the ball came out brilliantly that day. 'That's working well,' Jimmy said. 'That's good, that's working,' Sakes told me. 'I told you that you should have always bowled off that short run-up.' I thought, 'Fuck it. What have I got to lose? I'll just run in hard, attack the middle of the crease, and I won't be running for long enough to allow my feet to start crossing over. I might even bowl a bit quicker.' I only saw the upside.

I resolved to shave one-third of the distance off my run-up, bounding in from a standing start rather than taking a few paces to get up to full speed. Initially, it worked a treat. At Napier, I took 1 for 33 from my 10 overs as Jimmy ran through them at the other end; in the third ODI, roles reversed and I got the rewards. It felt great: I was bowling at 95mph again, I was taking wickets, and I was still opening the bowling. In between those two ODIs, the MCC announced the change that had been mooted for a while: rather than a dead ball, the umpires would give a no-ball if a bowler knocked the bails off at the non-striker's end moving forward. It was – and still is – a ridiculous law, in my opinion; the fact it's still referred to as 'Finn's Law' is not my proudest legacy.

In hindsight, what I failed to realise was that I hadn't just changed the distance I ran in, but the whole subconscious motion of my bowling: I had damaged the muscle memory that I had built up over more than a decade. The natural flow that is so integral for any fast bowler disappeared, because I had messed with the fundamentals. The things that had first caught Flower's attention and thrust me into the England team were gone: walking beyond my mark, looping round into my mark, and then gathering my stride towards the crease. I went from a bouncy run-up with long, flowing strides to short, jerky ones with no rhythm. The natural figure of eight – the thing that made me myself – was gone. I wish that I'd bowled a poor first spell in Napier, or had sprayed it everywhere in the nets and written it off as a failed experiment; instead, I stuck with it.

All I saw was the fact that I was bowling seriously quick and with great control: it felt like I had discovered a hidden hack that would turn me into one of the best in the world. Mike Selvey from the *Guardian* asked me whether I thought I could become the first England bowler to hit 100 miles per hour, and there were a flurry of speculative articles written on the back of that. It was outlandish, not least because Jimmy – as the senior bowler – would have first choice of ends, which usually meant that I could be running up a hill or into the wind, but I decided that I would keep using the short run-up in the Test series and see how things went. I could always revert back to the long run if I needed to, but wanted things to keep going as well as they were.

It was a risk, but it felt like a calculated one: I'd bowled well in those last two ODIs, and the fundamentals of my bowling plans didn't change across formats. Why shouldn't it work in the Tests too? I took the new ball at Dunedin, which felt like a vindication of how well things were going for me. I'd opened the bowling ahead of Broady in one-day cricket for a while, but this was the first time I'd done it in a Test match. The only problem was that there was nothing in the pitches, and we had to graft seriously hard.

For the only time in my career, it was my batting that made headlines in Dunedin. We'd been rolled cheaply in the first innings but Cook and Nick Compton got us up towards parity on the fourth day. I walked in as nightwatchman with two overs remaining, and it wasn't until the final session on day five that the Kiwis finally got me out. I eked out 56 off 203 balls, and couldn't stop smiling when I raised my bat – borrowed from KP, blank and stickerless, because I was between two bat sponsors – to mark the first half-century of my professional career.

I only ever wanted two things as a batsman: to have a solid enough defence that it was hard to get me out, and to show no weakness to the opposition. I could hold a bat – I occasionally scored a few runs playing club cricket – but since starting in the Middlesex Academy, I was used to being down the order.

I neglected my batting from a young age, because all I ever wanted to do was bowl, bowl and keep bowling. But I knew that I would still have a role to play: in my first Test summer, I made 9 not out off 50 balls to see Prior through to his hundred against Pakistan at Trent Bridge, and could see how much both he and the team appreciated me for it.

There was a fear factor in international cricket that I hadn't felt playing for Middlesex, but I knew that I could intimidate people with my own pace, too. It was scary as a young player, but I worked a lot at playing the short ball with Graham Gooch, our batting coach, and decided on that simple game plan: stay in line, and don't show any vulnerability. Some tailenders would back away to the leg side and try to get their body out of the way of the ball, but that wasn't my style: I resolved to get in line, and if the ball was going to hit me, I'd rather just wear it than suggest to the opposition that England's big, intimidating fast bowler was actually just soft. I always enjoyed the nickname that I earned for my over-my-dead-body defensive batting: the Watford Wall.

My efforts with the bat were well rewarded. I'd only just taken over as nightwatchman from Jimmy, who promised me a case of wine if I made it through to the lunch interval. Cooky heard him and pledged the same, and they said they'd double it if I could make it through to tea. I walked off on 56 not out with a big grin, and arrived home a few weeks later with a year's supply of red waiting for me. Cooky was true to his word; Jimmy's cases must have got lost in the post.

But my batting couldn't obscure the fact that I didn't do myself justice with how I bowled at Dunedin, and the second Test at Wellington wasn't much better: rain near enough wiped out the last five sessions, and while we made New Zealand follow on, Broady outbowled me. He was back to his best with his injury troubles behind him, taking six-for in the first innings; for their second innings, he took the new ball ahead of me again. The conditions weren't helpful, on flat, slow pitches, but I didn't feel quite right: my short run-up made everything feel too rushed in my action, and I kept on pushing the ball in towards the right-handers' pads.

Bad habits were creeping in. The jerkiness of my run-up meant that the path of my bowling arm became short; I was no longer using my long limbs to my advantage. At Eden Park in Auckland, where we played the third Test, Flower and Saker took me into the coach's room, an offshoot from the big rugby dressing rooms. They showed me some footage on a laptop, and Flower paused it.

'Why the fuck is the seam pointing towards first slip?' he asked me. I wanted to become the complete fast bowler, and because I didn't feel threatening on such a flat pitch, I was experimenting with other modes of dismissal; I thought I could swing the ball away from the right-handers at pace to have them caught behind or in the slip cordon. Flower was having none of it. 'That's what Broad and Anderson are in this team to do,' he barked. 'You are in the team to nip it back into right-handers and run it across the lefties.' It was frustrating: he was finally admitting that he saw me as having a different role to the rest of the bowling attack as his 90mph weapon, but without giving me the licence to really attack. There was no sense of a trade-off between runs and wickets as a result of my pace: I was still expected to be a strike bowler, but knew I'd be dropped if I consistently went at more than three runs per over.

I'd taken an expensive six-wicket haul in the first innings, but changed my grip as a result of that conversation for the second. I started holding the ball wobble-seam, not trying to swing it at all, and that in turn messed with where my wrist was. It was another small change with bigger repercussions than I realised at the time. My bowling action had always felt so natural to me, and I was ruining it: I thought I was making small tweaks, but each one had unintended consequences that were far bigger than that. As we left New Zealand with a nil-nil draw, thanks to Prior and Monty Panesar's fifth-day rearguard, I could tell that something wasn't quite right. It was only much later that I realised just how much I had stuffed myself up.

# 6

# Out of Control

I walked off the pitch at Edgbaston, up the stairs into the away changing rooms, and stormed off into the bathrooms. Whenever I was frustrated with how I'd bowled in a spell, I would go back into the dressing room and go bananas for a couple of minutes – rather than showing all of my emotions on the field – and then head back on to the pitch. But this time was different: rather than anger, I felt confused, flat and an overwhelming sadness. I sat inside the showers long enough for the motion-sensor lights to flick off and cried, for the first time that I could remember in my professional career, wondering why the skill that I thought I had started to master had suddenly deserted me.

With every ball that Jonathan Trott and Ian Bell clipped off their pads for singles into the leg side, the more helpless I felt: 'What is going on here?' Things were happening that I just couldn't explain. I couldn't locate the control that I'd had so recently: it felt like I no longer had command over what was happening. Control was the thing that I had spent my whole career craving, and I felt incredibly vulnerable without it. We were a week out from the first Test of the 2013 summer against New Zealand, and playing Warwickshire was an important benchmark for me: they were defending county champions, and bowling to two England teammates would tell me what level I was at heading into a huge year. The answer was confronting: I bowled 22 wicketless overs, and couldn't wrap my head around why the ball wasn't landing where I wanted it to.

I'd had a rare break at the end of the New Zealand tour, stopping off in Fiji on the way home. It was the only way that I could physically stop myself from bowling: if I'd spent two weeks off in London, I would have found a way to go and practise somewhere. I overlapped with a couple of friends out there but spent my twenty-fourth birthday solo on the other side of the world, enjoying the opportunity to relax and switch off. For the first time since I'd started playing for England, I could finally get away from cricket. In the eighteen months from October 2011 to April 2013, I'd made fifty international appearances across the formats, more than any other England player, and had been involved in every squad; that winter, I'd played every game that I was available for. It was the only lifestyle I knew, but such an intense way to live. My late return meant I only had three Championship matches to play before the first Test of the summer – maybe I could have gone to the IPL after all, rather than having to bowl for my place – and I started with six wickets off my short run-up in our win against Derbyshire at Lord's.

Even though I knew that something wasn't quite right, I thought I would simply bowl my way back into rhythm after the time off that I'd had. In 2010, when I'd been pulled out of the middle of the summer for my strengthening programme, my first game back was against Sussex at Uxbridge and I bowled unchanged for a whole session to try and find my groove again. I went through that natural flow of the figure of eight, again and again and again, and started to feel that fluidity coming back. I tried to do the same against Surrey at Lord's – opening the bowling to my old nemesis Graeme Smith – but I just couldn't find it.

The shorter run-up meant I had no flow, no natural rhythm in the sequence of my bowling. I'd sprint into the crease, really tense. Off my longer run, everything felt right: my arms would feel natural and long: I had that lovely fluid motion of going up, and then everything coming down, flowing towards the batter. It just wasn't there off the short run. I didn't bowl well in our first innings, and was pushing everything into the pads rather than standing it up off the seam. I went out to sit on the balcony with Angus Fraser and Richard Johnson on the second day, when it was our turn to bat, and hoped that they might have some ideas as to how I could get back to how I had bowled in those ODIs in New Zealand, consistently hitting 90mph and taking wickets for fun.

Gus turned to me and asked plainly, 'What have you done?' My heart sank. I already knew he and Jono weren't huge fans of the short run, but this felt like a major intervention. 'You don't look like yourself when you're bowling,' he told me. 'We don't like the look of this at all. You have to go back to your long run before it's too late.' Part of my brain was telling me to ignore Gus. I'd bowled so well off the short run to begin with, when it had felt like the magical change that would take my bowling from good to world-class. But the feeling in my chest told me that he was right – and on reflection, he definitely was. Deep down, I knew that this new action felt alien to me: the problem was that I didn't have much time to rediscover my old one. The penny dropped. It was the first time I sat there and thought, 'What do I do now?'

I went back to my longer run-up in the second innings,

as Smith knocked off Surrey's target pretty quickly, but my rhythm didn't return immediately. Things still felt rushed at the crease, and I was still pushing too many balls in. I had the horrible feeling that comes with a race against the clock: the first New Zealand Test was two weeks away. After that, we had the Champions Trophy, then the Ashes at home, then a one-day series against the Australians which I'd probably be expected to play in, then the away Ashes that followed. What I needed was a bit of time away from competitive cricket: a training block, where I could work out what had happened to my bowling action and focus on process rather than outcome. Instead, I had eight months of intense, relentless international cricket staring me in the face.

I stuck to the longer run-up at Edgbaston, and was expecting to just go back to being the bowler that I'd been at the end of the previous summer. But I couldn't get it to click. I couldn't get the ball to land where my brain was telling it to, and I couldn't understand why I wasn't rediscovering the rhythm that I felt I should be. One of the coaching staff came up to me after the third day and said: 'Just go out and get pissed tonight. I don't care if you turn up tomorrow and bowl hung-over: go and have a night out, and try to forget about everything that is going on inside your head.' I ignored him: I get anxious when I'm hung-over, and I didn't want to exacerbate the feeling of being out of control any more than I needed to. But the sentiment was right: I was overthinking everything, and people who were close to me in the changing room could see how much pressure I was heaping on myself to get things right.

I was so conscious of the fact that something was off that I started overthinking to a damaging extent. Over the winter, I'd had a one-point checklist of things to think about when I was bowling: keep your left arm close to your hip. That was it. It's easy to keep your mind clear when things are going well for you. After reverting to the long run-up, I was thinking about every single little thing that I did when I bowled. Was my stride length right? Did my cheeks feel floppy when I ran? How close was I to the stumps on release? Could I feel the flick of the ball off the end of my fingertips? It was a vicious cycle: every time I thought about a new aspect of my action, I felt something wrong somewhere else. Every time I'd have a net, I'd write something new down and my checklist would gradually get longer and longer and longer.

It wasn't as simple as just flicking back from short to long. It sounds like it should be incredibly straightforward: how hard can it be to just go back to what you were doing before? But think of it as trying to stretch back out a jumper that you've shrunk in the wash: there's no quick fix which makes things go back to normal. I'd built up that muscle memory of my run-up and my bowling routine over more than a decade, and the short run had thrown all of that off: I had lost the natural flow which is such a key component of fast bowling, and disrupted the core feeling of rhythm that I had when I reached the crease. At my best, I could just unfurl and bowl fast without having to think about what was going where; now every motion I made required an active thought.

The first Test arrived before I was ready, and I tried to give myself some positive reinforcement in the build-up. I was still only twenty-four, and I knew my record – 80 Test wickets at 29 – was still good. I was getting into the team on merit, and had earned my spot as the third member of our seam attack, alongside James Anderson and Stuart Broad.

**14 May 2013**

Simplicity and clarity of thought

    Get into a battle with the batsmen

    Left arm strong and into hip

    Attack the crease

Be aware of other things but concentrate on the above

You're a good fucking bowler

    Stats

    Attributes

    PACE

    BOUNCE

    INTIMIDATING

I'm aware of this frustration, BUT I AM OK

I am aware of this embarrassment, BUT I AM OK

Trust and believe in natural instinct.

It was all well and good writing it down, but once you're actively having to tell yourself to keep things simple and to clear your thoughts, you're already halfway to losing the battle. I bowled OK in that first Test – 4 for 63 in a convincing win – but I didn't feel myself again. I still had that happy knack of taking wickets, and polished off their lower order with the old ball, but I felt a bit all over the place: I didn't quite have the same rhythm, flow, pace or zip as I had nine months previously, when I'd bowled that brilliant spell to the South Africans at the same ground.

I met my parents afterwards and my mum went, 'That was pretty shit.' Honest feedback, usually my dad's speciality. I was pissed off. I thought, 'You've just had three days in Lord's hospitality for free thanks to me, and you're telling me I bowled crap?' It was Dad's glass that was usually half-empty like that: he could be in a beautiful room of a huge house and the first thing he'd notice would be a tiny blemish on the skirting board. It's just the way he's wired, and I'm sure that was an influence on my own perfectionism. I always respected my parents' opinions as they would tell me what they thought without a filter. I just wasn't ready to be confronted with the truth.

It was another sign in the first half of that summer that things weren't right. People close to me, who cared about me, were trying to tell me what they could see plainly and clearly, and I was trying to block it all out. There were all these things coming into my psyche that hadn't really been there before. It was affecting me. I was simultaneously becoming more introspective, and thinking about the details of my action, while kidding myself that I could just bowl my way out of it. The problem was that the more I bowled, the more I compounded the bad habits that had crept into my action; that in turn meant I felt even more out of control, and even less confident than I had done at the end of the previous summer.

The thing that I feared the most was that I was going to throw away my opportunity. I had bust a gut to get myself back into the team. I'd put in the hard graft and felt like I deserved to be there. But one stupid decision – bowling off that short run-up in New Zealand – had messed everything up for me. I wasn't catastrophising just yet, but things were starting to snowball. I tried to convince myself that I was one day, one training session, away from rediscovering my best. I bowled OK in the second Test, which we also won, and headed into the Champions Trophy thinking I wasn't too far away, despite a frustrating shin injury.

But for the opening match at Edgbaston, against Australia, I was left out. I was fuming. Ashley Giles had taken charge of the one-day team during the winter and had seen me bowl well in India and New Zealand, opening the bowling ahead of Broady. But for the start of the Champions Trophy, he decided to fiddle with the balance of the side: Ravi Bopara came in as an allrounder, and Tim Bresnan pipped me to the role of third seamer. I was spewing: I was still number 3 in the ICC's ODI rankings, and was desperate to play. For all that I wasn't bowling at my best, I had worked so hard to earn that spot over the previous two years, and as soon as a major tournament came around – on home soil, to make things even worse – I was running the drinks. I was rarely like that through most of my career, because I generally understood that it was the nature of the sport. But at that Champions Trophy, I was incredibly frustrated.

I was wound up even more by a comment that Gilo made to me. 'You're sulking and it's detracting from everything,' he told me after our win. 'Why can't you just be more like Woakesy?' Don't get me wrong: Chris Woakes is one of the nicest people you'll ever meet. He would become a battle-hardened international cricketer who achieved so much with the three lions on his chest, and deserves to go down as one of the best seam bowlers to play for England across formats. But at the time, he was finding his feet in international cricket and wouldn't have been one to make a scene if he wasn't playing. He just got on with his job of twelfth man – which I felt I had done, just without a smile. Not only had Gilo dropped me, he was now telling me off for being pissed off about it. 'Fuck him,' I thought, and went out into the centre of Birmingham determined to get blind drunk and forget about everything that was going on in my head.

My memories of that night are hazy, beyond a vague flashback of sitting on the street corner by myself and Jos Buttler coming to find me. We had been at Walkabout, an Aussie bar on Broad Street, and a few of the Australia squad were in there too – including David Warner, my old mate from our Middlesex days whom I had texted and told to come along. That turned out to be a big mistake. Jos dragged me to another bar, and soon after I was arm in arm with Gilo making up. 'I'm only saying this because I want the best for you,' he told me. 'I know, I'm just so disappointed that I'm not playing,' I said. I was so out of it that Trotty's wife Abi had to convince the hotel security that I was a guest when I was being put to bed at the end of the night. It was only the next morning that I heard the details of what had gone on in Walkabout, with Warner picking a fight with Joe Root and landing a punch on him. Cricket Australia suspended and fined him; in retrospect, it was an embarrassing night all round.

I played in our win over South Africa in the semi-final, when Bresnan was unavailable, and had Hashim Amla caught behind early. But I was left out again for the final, a narrow defeat to India in a rain-affected game. The Champions Trophy is a strange tournament: it felt like it would be a big deal to win, because of England's poor record at ICC events, but it didn't have the same prestige as a World Cup. Perhaps the strangest aspect is the white jackets presented to the winning team. The day before the final in Birmingham, a tailor came and measured us all up for blazers in a silky white material, but because we lost, we didn't get ours, and watched India slip them over their bright blue playing kit as they lifted the trophy. There must be a 2013 Champions Trophy winners' blazer made to measure for my specifications out there somewhere, but I've never got my hands on it.

Spending most of June running the drinks meant that I felt undercooked when we arrived in Nottingham for the first Ashes Test. I knew that I was battling to keep my place.

'There's no chance you're playing five Tests here unless you hit the ground running,' I told myself. But I made a strong start. We were bowled out cheaply on the first day, and with Broady off the field with a shoulder injury, I opened the bowling in an Ashes Test for the first time in my career. I took two wickets in two balls in my second over: Shane Watson, whom I usually found incredibly tough to bowl to, and Ed Cowan, both edged me into the slips. I was bowling with good pace, and felt like I had some rhythm off my longer run.

But it soon disappeared: we had a horrible second day, getting flogged around Trent Bridge by Phil Hughes and Ashton Agar, whose 98 not out was the highest score by a Test number 11, and I didn't have anywhere near the level of control that Andy Flower always demanded from his bowlers. I bowled one good spell of reverse swing in the second innings, troubling Steve Smith and Michael Clarke, but it was becoming clear that Alastair Cook was losing his faith in me. On the last day, I bowled only two out of 39.5 overs as Australia got close to pulling off their run chase, and Brad Haddin really got stuck into my bowling – just like he had in the 2010/11 series. The only Australian who sledged me was James Pattinson, the young fast bowler. His partnership with Haddin took Australia close on the final day, and every time I ran past him – either when I was bowling, or running near him in the field – he would let me have it.

It was an amazing Test match, one of the best I'd been involved in. Australia edged closer and closer, and only needed 20 more to win at lunch on the final day. I had a half-chance to win it just before, sprinting in off the square leg boundary and diving forward as Haddin swept one down towards me off Graeme Swann's bowling, but I couldn't quite cling on. Thankfully, Anderson was unbelievable, taking five wickets in each innings, and bowled a 13-over spell on the final day. He had Haddin caught behind to clinch a 14-run win, and it was an amazing feeling in the huddle when he was given out on review to give Jimmy his 10-for and us an early lead in the series. We'd been big favourites heading into the series, but Australia ran us seriously close. There was an incredible atmosphere at Trent Bridge and it was a win worth celebrating, but my performance hardly merited it: two wickets in 25 overs, and an economy rate of nearly five runs per over. 'You nearly fucked this win up,' I told myself.

I took my frustration out on myself: I peeled off from the celebrations, walked around the ground at Trent Bridge and went to the gym. I wanted to get all of my pent-up anger out: what better way to do that than a heavy weights session? Flower was livid when I came back to the dressing room. I'd done a lot of gym work over the last three years, and was physically stronger than I was when I first came into the England team as a stick-thin twenty-year-old. He wasn't convinced that it was good for me, and had a theory that it might be contributing to my problems: my limbs were no longer as loose and flowing as when he'd first watched me bowling for the Lions in early 2010. But quite simply, he was annoyed at me for leaving my teammates after a win like that, which he rightly thought we ought to have celebrated as a collective unit. It was another warning sign, in a year filled with them.

When we got to Lord's, I knew I was struggling to keep hold of the place that I had worked so hard to make my own. The day before the game, I was bowling out in the middle during a training session, and Flower came over to stand as the umpire. He gave me instructions as to where I should bowl: 'I want you to nip this one into the right-hander' or 'shape this one away from the outside edge'. It was a test to see if I could deliver that ball where I wanted it to, and I failed it spectacularly. I'm not sure any bowler could have nailed Flower's exact specifications – maybe Anderson in his absolute pomp would have managed – but I was missing by a long way. I sprayed a few miles down the leg side; I tried to bowl one full outside off stump which came out back of a length, straight. My mind was scrambled: with every ball I bowled that didn't go in the right place, I'd beat myself up more, and put myself in an even worse place to get the next one right. I was desperate to play an Ashes Test at my home ground, and came away feeling utterly dejected.

I was told later that day that I had been left out, with Bresnan replacing me, but England's style at the time was to keep things hush-hush until the last possible moment; the idea was that giving the team away ahead of the toss was handing unnecessary information to your opposition, and allowing them extra time to prepare. On the morning of a game, some players will get out of the dressing room early and have a bowl before the full team warm-up; I'd usually be out there having a stretch or kicking a football around at that time. I wasn't in the headspace to go through the motions that morning, so didn't bother; I knew I had to come out for the team warm-up and trudged out there in my trainers just before it started.

Flower marched over: 'Why the fuck are you wearing trainers?' I went, 'Well, I'm not playing, am I?' He snapped back: 'Australia don't know that. But if they see you wearing your trainers instead of your spikes, they will.' I turned on my heels, sprinted up to the dressing room, and changed into my spikes, then sprinted back down for the warm-up. Barely fifteen minutes later, Cooky announced our change at the toss: Finn out, Bresnan in. Flower was so hot on those small things, and his attention to detail was one of the key components of our rise to number 1 in the world. But at times, it could also come at the cost of man management: the last thing I needed on the day I'd been dropped partway through a series – for the second Ashes in a row – was a bollocking from my coach for wearing the wrong footwear.

It was one of several strange moments on a surreal day: Queen Elizabeth II was at Lord's, and both teams lined up in front of the pavilion to meet her. We were told before to address her as 'Your Majesty' and then call her 'ma'am' after that: ma'am like ham, not ma'am like palm. Cooky took her along the line of players, introducing each of us, and I was right at the end. 'This is Steven Finn,' he told her, and I was still so pissed off at being dropped that I forgot everything that I'd been told. 'Morning!' I said cheerily, almost immediately realising that I'd completely fluffed my lines on the first and last time that I would ever interact with the Queen. My parents have a framed photo of me shaking her hand that is the first thing you see as you walk in their front door. I laugh every time I see it, knowing that I said completely the wrong thing.

Straight after that interaction, I jumped in my car and drove to Brighton. This was the weirdest aspect of being dropped by England: not only did you have the disappointment of being left out but you were then expected to channel that by going straight back to your county and proving why you should have been selected. It happened to me a few times in the 2011 summer, when I only played one Test, and I remember racing down the motorway from Nottingham to London so that I could get to Lord's in time for the second session of a Championship game against Derbyshire. I had to warm up in the Long Room, and then trapped Wes Durston lbw in the first over that I bowled. I'd have *Test Match Special* on the radio while I was driving, listening to the commentary of a match I generally thought I should have been playing in, and would then arrive at a county game and have to jump straight into bowling. It felt normal at the time, but looking back, there were so many contrasting emotions to deal with. Thankfully, we were batting all day at Hove, but Luke Wright scored a really good hundred the next day; I tried to channel my frustration by bowling bouncers at him, running down the slope at Hove, but went at more than four an over.

For the third Test, I was left out of the squad altogether. All that hard work winning my spot back to play six Tests in a row, and all of a sudden, I was totally out of England's thinking. It hurt. My ambition had been to play ten Ashes Tests out of ten, but midway through the home series, I was playing 40-over matches for Middlesex and feeling a million miles away from my England teammates. I didn't put a date on them, but around the time I was dropped, I scrawled down some notes about what I should be doing when I bowled. They give an indication as to what was going on in my head, and the ever-growing checklist that I was developing; rather than running in with a clear mind, I was hyper-conscious of everything that I was doing.

Mid Ashes when dropped
    Strides to crease
    Starting on right foot with good momentum into mark
    Stay inside white line during run-up
    Attack my two white lines at crease
    Arms high and long – use levers
    Look at target
    Pull left arm into hip at crease

Complete action
Sounds like a lot but it's very simple
Straight lines to the crease make everything more
manageable
Remember – you're a fucking good bowler.

I started to catastrophise when I was left out of squads for the last three Tests. What if that's me done forever? What if I never get back into this team? How have I gone from opening the bowling in Wellington earlier this year to not even being good enough to run the drinks any more? Will I lose my England central contract, and the perks that come with it? I was starting to fear the worst, and knew that I desperately needed to sort out my bowling action. I had extra sessions with Kevin Shine, the ECB's lead bowling coach, to try and strip everything back to base principles.

At one point that summer, I was staying with my new girl-friend's family down in Devon, and met Shiney and Richard Johnson at a random cricket club in Bristol where there was a second-team game going on. People must have looked at me and wondered what on earth I was doing there, but I was determined to sort things out and wanted to work as hard as possible. I always felt I could be quite experimental with those two: we explored my run-up, various different grips, and the flow through the crease that I was craving. I came away from that session feeling like I'd made some progress, and like my run-up was getting back to where I wanted.

After missing the celebrations when we went to number 1 in the world two years previously, I decided that I was going to make it to the presentation at The Oval at the end of the Ashes. It was a strange old series. We won 3–0, but expectations were so high after back-to-back wins in 2009 and 2010/11 that we didn't get a whole lot of credit. Maybe it was because we knew there was another one to follow straight after, or maybe because there was a sense that Australia were no longer the force they once were. But the press were on our backs for playing boring cricket, and the feeling was that winning alone was no longer enough. Everyone knew that the true challenge would be backing up our previous win in Australia.

The celebrations were strange. I felt out of place, having played one Test out of five – I hadn't even been in the squad for the last month of the series – but nobody was getting carried away. I had to get myself up for it, but I'd regretted not being there to lift the mace given the part I'd played in it. I always had an appreciation of just how special the Ashes is as a series, so even though I'd only taken two expensive wickets in the series, I decided I was going to be part of it. Woakesy made his debut in the fifth Test, and there's a nice photo of us together: old Under-19s teammates, who had graduated to an Ashes-winning team. I took a couple of pictures for Kev on his phone, and even gave him a piggyback at one stage as we took it all in with the fans. But I was a peripheral figure: I drove down to the ground and didn't have a beer because I was playing for Middlesex the next day. Kev asked if I was sliding off, and I ended up giving him a lift home: a second Ashes win at the age of twenty-four, and I was the designated driver.

I played in some of the white-ball games against Australia at the end of the summer, and I bowled quickly. I hit 90mph at Durham in a T20, and I felt OK. It still wasn't perfect, but I wasn't fearing the worst: I knew that I would have times in my career where things didn't feel 100 per cent, and it was just a case of managing that. Under the surface, I knew that something was bubbling away – there was something going on that I couldn't control. But there was another Australia tour looming, so I didn't want to admit any weakness to myself. As I saw it, the only way to get through this blip was to keep pushing myself harder and harder until everything clicked. Ripping things up and starting from scratch was never a consideration: I was belligerent and stubborn, and wanted to focus on the future rather than the past.

I was trying to figure everything out on the job; trying to recalibrate myself. My numbers for Middlesex – and for England in the white-ball series that I played in – were solid enough, without me bowling the house down. I knew that I wasn't bowling as well as I had done twelve months previously, but it's not like I was a complete mess: in my final game of the home summer, I took 2 for 43 in an ODI win against Australia, getting Aaron Finch and Michael Clarke out lbw. A couple of weeks later, I was named in the touring party for Australia and I still felt like I could push my case to get back in the side. Nobody had nailed down that third seamer spot in my absence, and Bresnan was ruled out of the start of the tour with an injury. The selectors took me, Chris Tremlett and Boyd Rankin down to Australia as tall, hit-the-deck bowlers who could help us replicate the success that we'd had three years previously.

It might sound crazy, knowing how things panned out, but I felt genuinely confident that we would go down there and win – and that I could play a big part in the series. Australia hadn't come close to us in England. I knew the conditions would level things out a little bit, but the cracks under the surface in our team hadn't yet become obvious. As I saw it, we had an amazing batting line-up that would churn out big totals on good batting pitches, and with Broad, Anderson and Swann, we had the core of an attack that could take 20 wickets in every Test. I was one of several options for the final bowling spot, and whoever was picked would be in good enough form to support everyone else. It was never a consideration that we would struggle, let alone to the extent we did.

# 7

# Rock Bottom

I was getting desperate. As the flight to Australia for the 2013/14 Ashes tour drew closer into view, I still wasn't feeling like myself when I bowled. I was getting deeper and deeper inside my own head, focusing on every tiny detail of my bowling action. My bowling checklist grew longer and longer: run straight through the crease. Keep your arms as 'long' as you can. Maintain your stride length. Arms high in your bound. Use your levers. Bring your front arm close to your hip. Feel the energy of your fingertips. It wasn't that these tips were without merit, but I was overloading myself with information. I tried to convince myself that there was a world where I could remember all of them – let alone process them – every time I ran in and bowled. It was hopeless: like any bowler, I was at my best when I kept things simple, and I was massively overcomplicating.

I was training at Middlesex's indoor school in Finchley in the build-up to the tour, and after I'd finished bowling for the day, would head downstairs to the LA Fitness for a gym session. I enjoyed pushing myself in the gym, and had become a much stronger man than the lightweight boy who first played for England, but I started to take things a bit too far. My routine at the time was a weights session, followed by a cycle on an exercise bike, and I would keep on pushing after finishing what I was meant to be doing. I convinced myself that my work ethic was what set me apart, and was the thing that would get me back to my best after a shitty summer.

In one session, I pushed myself so hard physically on the bike that my legs literally wouldn't turn over any more. I stared at myself in the mirror with gritted teeth, and told myself: 'You're not a pussy. You're not weak. You're going to get through this.' I saw it as mentally preparing myself for what I wanted to do when I landed in Australia: turning up early for training, working harder than anyone else in the squad, and leaving no stone unturned as I tried to rediscover my form. I saw that single-mindedness as the attitude that champions had, rather than an unhealthy obsession that was taking over my life. I never had any escape from it; everything that I did became a competition to prove to myself that I wasn't weak.

There was no Bavarian boot camp before this Ashes tour, but Andy Flower organised a bizarre team-building exercise in Staffordshire instead. He got on well with a guy named Floyd Woodrow, an SAS soldier turned motivational speaker, and they set up a three-day reconnaissance mission: we were given surveillance training, then had to track down some actors who were posing as criminals. The whole thing was surreal, and all the senior players were baffled. But I was still twenty-four, and was so determined to buy into everything that the team wanted from me that I ended up being put in charge of the whole thing on the final day. I had to brief everyone, oversee three or four different sub-groups, and make sure that we completed the tasks by reprimanding the right guys. To raise the stakes, we were told that if we didn't complete it, nobody would be allowed to go home that night.

I hardly slept. I wasn't in the best headspace already, but now I was ultimately responsible for whether or not guys who I'd toured the world with would be allowed to go home to their wives and kids. I was so stressed because I felt like I'd be letting people down if I got something wrong. Just like I had in the gym, I was beating myself up to the point of being unkind to myself, and heaping unnecessary pressure onto everything that I did. I was so desperate to prove to everyone – to Flower, to my teammates and to myself – that I was worthy, and was there to make a difference. Thankfully, the missions were deemed a success, but I went home feeling drained. Woodrow congratulated me for leading them, and told me I could have been good in the services; I resisted the temptation to tell him that I'd have been absolutely useless.

In isolation, a big gym session and one sleepless night might sound like nothing. But they were part of the bigger picture for me, which was that I was never giving myself a break. There was no opportunity to switch off or escape. There was hardly ever a gap in our England schedule long enough for me to have a week's holiday and recover from everything: there was always something coming around the corner that demanded my full focus. I find it so frustrating when I see pundits criticising athletes for not training enough, or having interests outside of their sport. At the top level, performance depends so much on being in the right headspace. My career was a perfect counterexample to the idea that you should just be practising and practising relentlessly all day: lacking an outlet or an escape was one of my biggest problems.

We arrived in Perth in late October, and I had more than three weeks to get myself right before the first Test at the Gabba in Brisbane. Hard work was my route back into the side, as I saw it. There would be two buses from the team hotel to training every morning: one for the coaches, who would go and set the session up, and one for the players, half an hour later. Every day, I'd be in with the coaches, travelling down early to do drills before then bowling in practice. It reflected the mindset and attitude of that England team under Flower: there was always someone waiting in the wings to take your spot, and you wouldn't dream of cruising through a training session or a warm-up game.

There is already enough pressure on any player on an Ashes tour without them loading even more on to themselves, but I continued to be incredibly self-critical. I'm sure the disappointment of being dropped mid-series in 2010/11 played a part, but I was hell-bent on winning my place back and beat myself up when things didn't go perfectly. *'Poor training session,'* I wrote in my diary on the third day of the trip. *'Floaty and poor lines. Felt like it did in the summer. Need to nip it in the bud.'*

There was a different feeling to the first few weeks of the trip compared to three years previously. In 2010/11, there were nights when the tour felt like a holiday. It wasn't that we weren't taking the cricket seriously – far from it – but we went out for drinks and dinner, had a laugh with one another, and enjoyed the fact we were in an amazing country. In 2013/14, the sole focus was winning. Flower was ruthless: he only cared about winning. He didn't care what it looked like; he didn't care if people were falling asleep in the stands watching us, so long as we won. It worked for a period of time but then wore thin. Maybe it was because priorities in life had shifted as guys got older, or maybe the novelty of being away from home had worn off after so many winters on the road, but I don't think anybody had much fun on that trip.

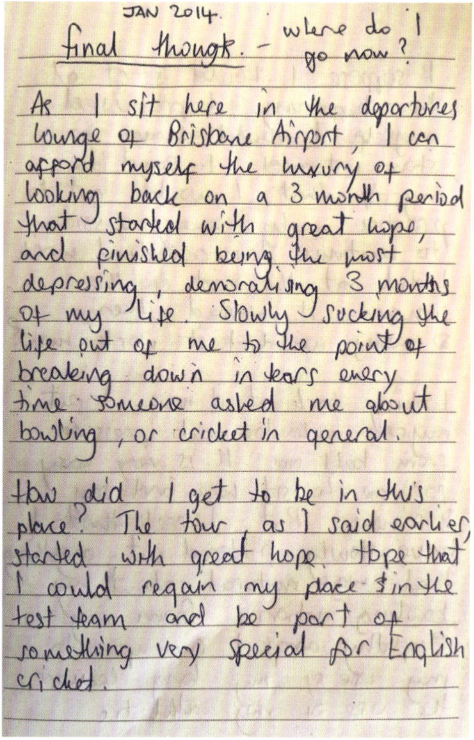

JAN 2014.

**final thought.** — where do I go now?

As I sit here in the departures lounge of Brisbane Airport, I can afford myself the luxury of looking back on a 3 month period that started with great hope, and finished being the most depressing, demoralising 3 months of my life. Slowly sucking the life out of me to the point of breaking down in tears every time someone asked me about bowling, or cricket in general.

How did I get to be in this place? The tour as I said earlier started with great hope. Hope that I could regain my place in the test team and be part of something very special for English cricket.

A page from my diary

My first Middlesex mugshot

Celebrating with Andrew Strauss during my spell in the Pro40 play-off

Receiving my first cap from Michael Atherton for my England Test
debut versus Bangladesh in March 2010 . . .

. . . and celebrating by taking wickets

May 2010: nine wickets against Bangladesh, including 5 for 87 in the second innings, to take my place on the Lord's honours board. As you can tell, I was happy

*Below* Prepping for my Ashes debut in the nets at the Gabba

Shushing the fan in the crowd at the WACA who had been giving me stick non-stop after taking the wicket of the late Phil Hughes

*Below* Celebrating with my good pal Eoin Morgan after wrapping up the series in Sydney

*Far below* 'Leave it, Finny, he's not worth it'

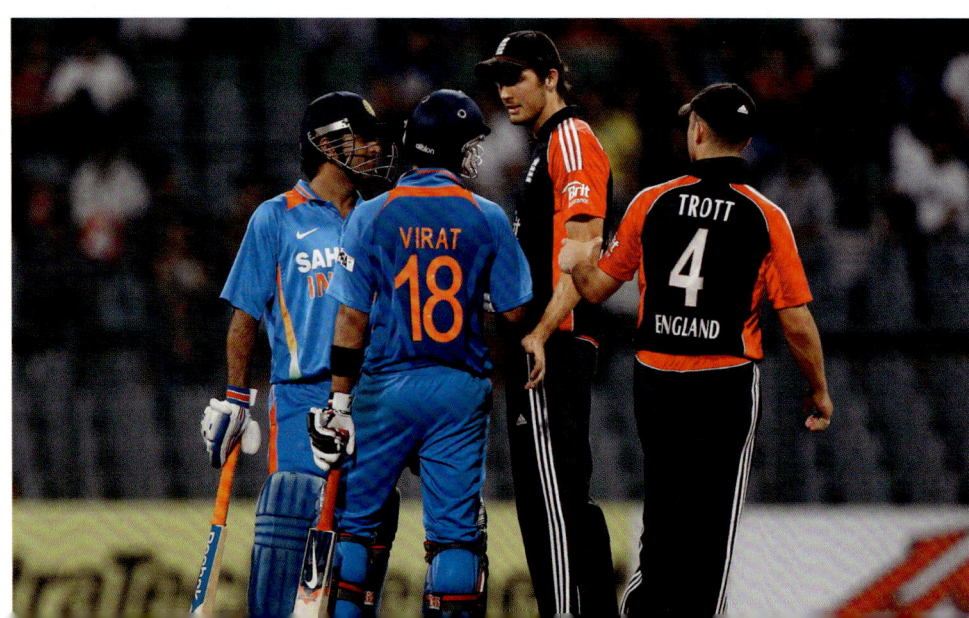

Headingley 2012: arguing with Steve Davis as my woes with kneeing the stumps begin

Taking the wicket of South Africa's Jacques Rudolph at Lord's during one of my best spells

The side-on angle from Alice Springs in 2013/14 which revealed the 'shortness' that had crept into my action

'Morning!'

One of my greatest moments: taking the wicket of Steve Smith during my third Test comeback at Edgbaston, July 2015 . . .

. . . and seeing off Adam Voges the day after

*Below* Leading the team off after the Edgbaston victory

*Far below* Celebrating with Moeen Ali and Jos Buttler after sealing the series win

Photographer Gareth Copley captured the exact moment Rob Young, the team doctor, told me I was ruled out of the 2015 series against Pakistan. I was devastated

*Left* Winning the County Championship with my boyhood club in 2016 was one of the happiest days of my career

*Below* I finally plucked up the courage to ask my hero Glenn McGrath for a photo during the 2021/22 Ashes tour

There were curfews in place at night, and Stuart Broad ended up on the back page of a newspaper when he went for a quiet drink at a bar during one of the warm-up games. The Australian press were out to get Broady on that tour after what had happened at Trent Bridge earlier in the year – when he stood his ground after umpire Aleem Dar somehow missed a huge outside edge – and tried to make his life a misery. Players were summoned by the management for interviews about who had been out the night before, and how many drinks they'd bought. It might have been the explosion of social media, which had become a much bigger thing, but there was no sense that we were there to enjoy the experience of an Ashes tour. It was win or bust.

Our first warm-up game against Western Australia went worse than I'd feared: Mitch Marsh and Ashton Turner both laid into me, and my figures in the first innings (1 for 123 in 23 overs) were less than ideal. I tried to stay calm – I hadn't started the tour brilliantly in 2010/11 either – but alarm bells were ringing. It was roasting hot, and there were massive blue-bottle flies in my face. My biggest fan from the 2010/11 tour was there to keep me company, too. 'I haven't forgotten you, Finn!' he yelled from the members' stand, three years after I had 'shushed' him celebrating a wicket. 'You were shit on the last tour, and you're still shit now.' This time, he might have had a point. I was trying to bowl relatively full, because the WACA is such a bouncy pitch that you have to get it up there to hit the top of the stumps, but I kept on sending down low full tosses. The sense of no control that I dreaded was creeping back in: I was missing my length by a good distance, and was pissed off that I couldn't discover the feeling of bowling a good length. I wanted to bowl a spell which proved I meant business and was there to play a massive part in the series. This was anything but.

Kevin Pietersen took me aside for a chat on the second day of the game. He wasn't playing in the warm-up, but had watched a bit of the first innings and quickly identified that I was bowling with inhibitions. We were different personalities, but I always felt that Kev really believed in me as a bowler: he always rated me, dating back to my first tour in Bangladesh, and I felt as though he cared about me as a person, too. I loved watching him bat: he trained incredibly hard, but seemed to go out into the middle with the carefree mindset that I desperately wanted to rediscover. That day, he was trying to reassure me, reminding me that I was a good bowler and telling me that beating myself up all the time wouldn't solve anything: 'Mate, you just need to relax and let it happen.' I appreciated Kev looking out for me, but the fact that someone of his stature was asking me what was wrong in the first week of the tour should tell you just how far I was from my best.

I had a meeting with Flower, David Saker and Mark Bawden, the team psychologist, on the same day. They told me that it looked as though I wasn't trusting myself, which was painfully obvious. I resolved that my attitude should be, 'Fuck it.' 'Second innings, I HAVE to go with the "fuck it" approach,' I wrote in my diary. 'If a bad ball happens, I have to forget about it. Commit 100% to what I'm doing and trust what I have been doing. Bowl quick – it's what you're good at.' I felt slightly better in the second innings, but knew that I was a long way away from selection for the first Test.

I didn't play in the second warm-up match in Hobart, but was back for the last one in Sydney. It was my final opportunity to put my hand up for selection for the first Test, but I was still searching for control. My head was scrambled, filled with different ideas as to what was going wrong. I took some wickets in the first innings, but didn't bowl well: I sprayed the ball all over the place, and felt completely empty. The dressing rooms at the SCG were really old-school, and the ground has its own tradition: there was a wooden locker or wardrobe in the viewing area where any batters who scored hundreds, or bowlers who took five-wicket hauls, had to sign the door. This warm-up match was a first-class game, so the dressing room attendant had written, 'STEVEN FINN (ENG XI) vs CA INV XI, 28.4–4–103–5' and told me that I had to sign it. I felt like an imposter, not least when I saw Alastair Cook, Jonathan Trott and Matt Prior's names next to mine for their centuries in the final Test of the 2010/11 series. I reluctantly scrawled my autograph, and felt totally empty as I did it.

By the third day, I knew that my hope of playing in Brisbane was gone and I bowled even worse, with no control what-soever. *'SO SO SO FRUSTRATING,'* I wrote in my diary. *'Real poor opening spell. Bowled everywhere ... Nothing worse than the feeling of inadequacy and embarrassment. I can't let this happen to me any longer!'* There was no way that they could select me for the first Test at the Gabba, unless everyone went down with food poisoning on the morning of the game. I'd arrived in Australia convinced that I could get myself in a position to play, but I was miles away: I took wickets in that game, but if I was conceding four runs an over against a second-string team in a warm-up match, it could have been seriously ugly in a Test match.

My head was fried. My mum came out to Australia for the first two Tests, by herself, and I barely saw her. The problems I was having with my bowling had become all-consuming and I was embarrassed at the state I had got myself into. I didn't want her to realise that things weren't right, and I dealt with it by hiding away: I kept myself to myself and took her out to dinner once in the whole time she was there. One night in Brisbane, she had an allergic reaction. She was lying in her hotel room, struggling to breathe as her throat closed up, and came out with a rash all over her body. I only found out about it much later: she knew that I was struggling and didn't feel like she could disturb me while I was in the team environment ahead of an Ashes Test. What sort of person had I become that my mum didn't feel like she could ring me for help when she was in trouble? I feel awful thinking back to it, but it shows you the headspace that I was in. I didn't want to be out and about, or to engage with anyone; I just wanted to hide. I became incredibly self-conscious again. The hard thing about being away on tour is that there's no escape; every single day that you pull on an England training kit, there's someone watching you, whether it's at a cricket ground, a hotel lobby or an airport.

During the first Test, I was sent to go and train with the England Lions squad, who were in Brisbane shadowing the full tour. Flower and Saker knew I wasn't right, and thought that training away from the pressurised environment of the Test squad would help. They told me to go away and work hard on my bowling, because that was all they knew: all the leaders and senior players in that England team prioritised work ethic over anything else, and it was the trait they respected more than any other. People started to notice a deterioration in my mood, and the fact that I was starting to withdraw from social situations, but I wanted to seem as headstrong as possible. If Cooky, or a coach, asked me how I was doing, I'd say, 'Look, I'm having a hard time of it, but I'm just working as hard as I possibly can to get back into a state where you can pick me, and I can contribute to us winning the series.' I didn't want to admit any vulnerability, because I felt like I'd be stuffing myself; if I revealed how much I was struggling to anyone involved in picking the team, there was no chance that I'd be selected.

The Lions psychologist was a guy named Mike Rotherham, who came up to me after I'd bowled a couple of spells at batters in the nets at Allan Border Field. I was still feeling short of any sense of flow or rhythm, and hadn't bowled with any real consistency or snap; I was chuntering at the back of the nets, and berating myself. If I couldn't bowl at the Lions in the nets without feeling under pressure, how on earth could I hope to go into an Ashes Test match in front of tens of thousands of fans and do it? I clearly didn't look right, because Mike approached me and asked, 'Is everything OK?'

That question alone was enough to set me off, and the floodgates opened. All of the emotions that I had tried to keep in check came spilling out. I'd seen everything that was happening to me as a hurdle up to that point, but this was the first real block. How had I fucked things up so spectacularly? How had I gone from feeling like I was becoming one of the best fast bowlers in the world a year ago, to the point where I couldn't feel like myself bowling a cricket ball? Occasionally it would be there for a few balls, which made the whole process even more frustrating. I found it very easy to be unkind to myself. It wasn't by design, but that one question sparked something, and allowed me to be vulnerable for the first time and admit these emotions to myself. It must have been a strange sight for a young Lions player, thinking, 'What is the matter with this Finn bloke, bawling his eyes out to a psychologist because he's bowled a few dodgy overs in the nets?' But it was the first time that I truly revealed how I was feeling to anyone – including to myself.

**25 November 2013**

Never been so low at a training session. Cried to a bloke I've never even met before. Feeling of hopelessness and at my wit's end. Need to try and stop feeling like this.

Third spell was good – the zip and sting off the end of my fingertips came back. Important to remember how it feels when it's good, and try to replicate that. You can do it – just need to remember the feeling.

Chat with Cooky in the afternoon – trying/wanting to help. I don't have a magic solution, he said. Hard work and graft is the only way out of this.

It was no coincidence that I opened up to someone involved in the Lions camp, rather than the full England environment. I had a good relationship with Mark Bawden, the England team psychologist: we'd worked together in India on a hypnosis tape, where I'd record myself listing off all the things that made me a good bowler and listen back to it. But I didn't engage as I could have done with him: as far as I was aware, he was oblivious to the extent of what was going on inside my head. The problem was, I was wary of team psychologists: I could never quite shake the sense that they were too ingrained with the team to be truly impartial, particularly later on in my career. There was always that nagging doubt in the back of my mind, and I didn't want to admit my vulnerability to anyone in the dressing room. With hindsight, it wouldn't have happened because of the confidentiality that psychologists have, but I was paranoid that if I told him, 'Listen, Bawds, I'm stuffed here,' then he would relay it to Flower, and my Ashes hopes would be over. Really, I should have been brave and admitted how low I was feeling, how hopeless my situation felt and how much I was beating myself up every day.

The first Test was brutal. I watched it as twelfth man, and Mitchell Johnson's name was soon on everyone's lips. He had become a figure of fun for the Barmy Army in the past couple of Ashes series – 'He bowls to the left, he bowls to the right, that Mitchell Johnson, his bowling is shite' – but looked like a different bowler in the ODI series against us at the end of the 2013 summer, and completely blew us away at the Gabba: he took 9 for 103 in the match, and was bowling at the speed of light. Jonathan Trott was bounced out by him in both innings, and he made an incredibly brave decision to take himself out of the firing line, leave the tour and head home: he knew that he wasn't in the right headspace to perform, and desperately needed to give himself a break.

During our warm-up game in Sydney, we had trained inside during a rain delay in a dimly lit indoor centre. Trotty was training unbelievably hard by that stage: he had the bowling machine set at high pace, facing bouncer after bouncer after bouncer. He was getting absolutely peppered: hit on the gloves, hit in the armpit, hit on the head. It was a huge red flag that everyone ignored; we all just thought, 'It's Trotty. He's always practised hard.' I felt guilty when he went home. I considered myself one of Trotty's mates within that environment, but I was so self-absorbed and consumed by the shit that I was going through that I had never thought to ask him how he was. Everyone was already rattled by what had happened on the pitch, and Trotty's decision put us further on edge. The way that he batted was all about resilience; suddenly, one of the most resilient people I'd ever met had admitted his vulnerability to the world.

There was another practice game between the first and second Tests, and after such a heavy defeat at the Gabba, I knew that I was more than likely going to play so the other bowlers could rest. We were up in Alice Springs, in the Northern Territories, and it was the last practice match before the end of the series. I knew it was my last opportunity to find some rhythm in a match situation, so I heaped the pressure on myself, yet again. This was my chance. I had to get this right, and get it right now. It was now or never. All that did was compound my negative perception of myself, and my sense of worthlessness: I bowled 15 wicketless overs, conceded more than four runs per over, and felt like I'd bowled myself out of contention not only for the second Test in Adelaide but for the whole series.

The worst moment came when I saw a photo of myself from side-on, which revealed to me just how badly wrong my bowling action had become. At my best, I used the length of my arms to my advantage: as I saw it, the length of my levers helped to propel the ball as quickly as possible towards the far end. That nice long, smooth action I'd always had was what made me the bowler I was. But somehow, over the previous nine months, I had made everything short. My arm was beyond the perpendicular in this photo, taken a few split seconds before I was about to release the ball, and my arm was bent. It totally scrambled my head. I suddenly thought, 'Shit, that is so far away from what I am trying to do here. Why does my arm look like that? How has that happened?' I could see how tense I looked. That photo encapsulated everything I'd done wrong for the last ten months. I couldn't stop staring at it on my phone, wondering how I'd tangled myself up into such a mess.

Alice Springs has a tiny, two-runway, domestic-only airport, but Flower somehow found a quiet spot in the terminal there as we waited to get on the flight down to Adelaide. 'It's not happening for you,' he said. He told me that he wasn't going to consider me for selection for the second Test, and that I should spend the week working with Saker in the nets. 'We need you firing,' he told me. 'We'll need you at some point in this series, and I want you back at your best.' Immediately, I felt a huge sense of relief. I could stop worrying about pushing for selection, and had a bit of time to try and work things out on my own terms. I didn't have to cope with the fear of having to try and bowl in front of 50,000 people, or the prospect of embarrassing myself in front of millions on TV. Finally, I could take some pressure off myself. It showed me that for all his hard, militant exterior, Flower did care. Sure, he was harsh sometimes – to others, and to me. But deep down, there's a lovely man in there, which showed itself in that moment.

I had a good week down in Adelaide. I was excited to wake up early and head down to the nets to bowl with Sakes guiding me, and felt like I was on the right path to get back. Adelaide is a brilliant city, and Adelaide Oval is an amazing ground; I loved playing there in 2010, and playing an important role in our win on the final day, and finally felt at ease again. *'Really good in training,'* I wrote in my diary. *'Just to need to apply to a game now.'* It was only with hindsight that I realised the correlation between my best week of the tour and the absence of any stress about being in contention for selection. Everything felt so much better when the pressure was off. It's so frustrating to look back on. How on earth didn't I see it? Clearly, others around me were noticing it: even Flower, who had enough on his plate with Trotty heading home and us going 2–0 down in the series, had realised that I was putting myself under massive strain.

Everything came crashing back down in Perth. I thought I would just keep trying to groove the work I'd done in Adelaide, but being back in contention for selection did nothing to help my headspace. I was nowhere near making the final eleven, even though we'd been thrashed again in Adelaide, but being in consideration again meant that I was fretting again. *'Not so good training,'* I wrote. *'Feels like two steps forward and one step back.'* In reality, it was more like one forward and ten back.

I kept on working as hard as possible, and decided that I would take myself off to bowl in the nets at the WACA during the Test itself. I was there on my own with a bag of six balls, bowling at a stump in an empty net; I'd walk down to the far end, pick them all up, and walk back to the back of the net to do it all over again. It was schoolboy stuff, and all I was doing was compounding bad habits once again. During one of these sessions, Michael Clarke, the Australian captain, was in the next net over from me doing some work with a batting coach. I didn't know Clarke well, but he came up to me and asked what on earth I was doing. It didn't feel like he was being condescending, more inquisitive as to what was going on. He couldn't understand how what I was doing could possibly be beneficial to my bowling – and he was right. I couldn't see it at the time: I just thought I was training harder, demonstrating my work ethic, and doing all of the right things that would make it click.

There was a darker side to all of that extra work in Perth, which was where my mindset really started to take a turn for the worse. I was physically drained from bowling as much as I was, and was still doing extra running, gym work, you name it, to try and train my way out of this hole. I realised that I was in what physiotherapists call 'the red zone', when you are most likely to get injured; the thought crossed my mind that if I kept on bowling, I might injure myself just enough to get sent home. If I could strain my side or my quad, I could do myself a real favour, and stop putting myself through the torture that bowling day after day had started to become.

I couldn't see another way out. There was no finish line: I'd been named in the squads for the ODI and T20 series at the end of the Australia tour; after that, I'd be off to the Caribbean for a one-day tour, then over to Bangladesh for the World T20. I didn't feel like I could go up to the coaches and tell them, 'Look, I'm fucked here. I need a break.' It was a strange time because I was clearly still showing some signs that it wasn't far away: why would they keep picking me otherwise? That reinforced in my mind that the only way to potentially rediscover my zip was to keep pushing myself harder and harder. If that meant injuring myself, then so be it; at least I'd get a break.

Things have changed a lot in the decade since: I had so much respect for Ben Stokes when he pulled himself out of a Test series against India in 2021 to prioritise his mental health, but I never felt like that was an option available to me. Trotty's decision to come home from that same tour ended up helping to prompt a change in how people approached the mental side of the game, but at the time, it felt like he was getting nailed for it. It was huge news that was covered daily in an unkind way. I felt like doing that would have carried a perception that I was weak, or didn't care enough. I was a 24-year-old who had spent the last four years in an ultra-competitive environment: no wonder I didn't want to come across as weak. I didn't have any agency over what was happening to me: the control that I had always craved had never felt further away.

If the snowball of negative emotions was rolling down the hill in Perth – where we went 3–0 down in the series, surrendering the Ashes – it became a full-scale avalanche by the time we reached Melbourne. Everything was compounding to the extent that I felt totally out of control. People had started to pick up on the fact that things weren't right. The nets at the MCG are open-topped and claustrophobic: they are lower than the main concourse, and I felt like a goldfish in a bowl as I saw the eyes on me from the viewing gallery above. Bowling through to a stump at the WACA had felt like a safe space – at least, until Clarke called me out on it – because it's not that easy for fans to stand there and watch. I could bowl a shit delivery, and it wouldn't matter. But there were consequences again when the batters were back in the nets, preparing for the Boxing Day Test. An accidental bouncer had the potential to hurt one of my teammates, not to mention the embarrassment of my teammates realising just how much of a tangle I had got myself into. It was unavoidable to bowl at batters because the guys playing needed practice, but I felt like shit while bowling at them, so I hung around like a bad smell until everyone had gone through the nets then bowled by myself for half an hour more.

I felt completely lost. I was still presenting a hard exterior, and didn't properly open up to anyone. My then-partner had come out to visit, and more and more of my teammates were starting to ask if I was all right, but I just tried to shut myself off. I stopped writing in my diaries, too: writing things down and admitting my emotions to myself would have forced me to relive everything that happened for a second time in a day, when it had been painful enough the first time. I didn't feel present in anything I was doing: my mind was a fog, a daze of negative emotions. I had arrived in Australia feeling like I had an opportunity to prove to everyone – and particularly to myself – that what had happened in the summer was just a blip. As the series dragged on, and it became painfully obvious to me that I was in no fit state to play a Test match, I felt like everything had been completely stripped away from me, to the extent that I had no clue how I was ever going to feel like myself again. Fundamentally, I didn't want to admit that I had fucked everything up from where I had been the year before. I had the opportunity to do it all and have it all, and here I was bowling through to a stump by myself because I just wasn't good enough. I bottled those feelings up for years.

I had always been quite stubborn in a cricketing environment: if someone came up to me with an observation or some advice, I could quickly filter it out if I decided it wasn't important or relevant. As the tour wore on, I was so desperate for the golden bullet that was going to solve my issues that I was trying something different in every single training session. Flower came up to me at one point and said, 'Have you seen how Ryan Harris loads up?' He had a unique flick to get his wrist behind the ball, which I would suddenly find myself trying to imitate for a few balls. It wouldn't work, and I would be on to the next idea. What can I try now? What is suddenly going to make me feel like myself again? I reached the point where if a random member of the Barmy Army came up to me and said, 'I thought you were a bit wider on the crease in 2010; have you tried doing that again?' then I would try to implement it when I next bowled. I had no faith in anything I was doing and no concept of why I was doing it. I'd gone from being a stubborn, belligerent man to a vulnerable little boy who didn't have anything to fall back on.

I have been asked a few times if I had the 'yips' on that tour, but I don't think it's a helpful word. The mere mention of it sends shivers down any cricketer's spine. In a nutshell, I just didn't feel like myself. By changing my run-up earlier in the year I had messed with the fundamentals of what made me, me. I lost the zippy feeling on the end of my fingertips when I was bowling; my arm was bent in a place where it shouldn't have been; and I was nervous every time I bowled. I had so many different things running through my head that I became totally confused. When you're at your best, everything is happening subconsciously, but throughout the tour I was incredibly conscious of the motion of bowling. I couldn't get the ball to go exactly where I wanted it to, but it's not like I was missing the cut strip or bowling head-high beamers every ball. Does that qualify as the yips? I don't know, but it was never a word I used to describe it. I'm not sure that you can ever recover from them, and although I was struggling to work out my route back to being an England regular, I was determined that this wasn't going to be the end of my international career.

It won't surprise you to learn that I was nowhere near selection for the Sydney Test, even with England 4–0 down. Gary Ballance, Scott Borthwick and Boyd Rankin all made their debuts, which meant that we had used eighteen players in the series; Australia picked the same eleven the whole way through. I was the only man in our initial seventeen-man squad not to play a Test match, and two guys who weren't even named in that – Borthwick and Tim Bresnan, who recovered from injury – ended up jumping ahead of me. For the second Ashes tour in a row, I was in a unique position: I'd gone from being the only England player dropped in the 2010/11 series to being the only player not selected at all this time around. Once again, I was isolated and alone with my negative feelings. But my main response to missing out on selection again was simply, 'Thank fuck for that.' It already felt like public humiliation bowling in front of a handful of journalists and some passers-by in the nets; I can only imagine how I might have coped in front of nearly 50,000 people – and the TV cameras beaming it around the world.

A truly great England team was falling to pieces around me: Trott went home after the first Test, Graeme Swann retired after the third because his elbow was in pieces, and Flower's relationship with Pietersen had deteriorated to a new low. We were getting torn to pieces in the press and the mood was clearly not good, but I was still naive to the extent of what was going on behind the scenes on that tour. I was so deep inside my own head that when I turned up to training, I didn't give a moment's thought to who had been briefing what to whom, or whether KP had been whistling after a dismissal. Graham Gooch gave him a dressing-down when he was caught at long-on, and Kev bit back at him – but I didn't see it as anything deeper than two guys who really cared about England winning games. I hadn't had much experience of being part of a losing dressing room, but I just thought we were getting blown away by Mitchell Johnson and that everything would be back to normal the following summer as we looked to rebuild the team. Even when we were winning, there had occasionally been some natural friction within the dressing room: I didn't see anything out of the ordinary, beyond the fact that a team that was used to winning was suddenly getting hammered. It didn't ever dawn on me that this was the end of an era: my thought process was so insular that I didn't see the fires that had started to blaze around me.

I was given a rare day off from twelfth-man duties on the third day of the Sydney Test, and for once, I decided to be kind to myself; it was a chance to escape. I went to Milk Beach to try and switch off. I had no reception down there and when I finally got some signal again as I headed back towards the road to get a cab back to town, my phone blew up: I had a load of missed calls from Phil Neale, the team manager, and worked out pretty quickly that we'd been beaten even quicker than anyone had anticipated. I had to rush back to the team hotel to get back into my England-branded travel kit, and ended up missing the post-match presentation because I was in a taxi on the way to the SCG. There were roadblocks around the ground which meant I couldn't just be dropped off at the gates, and found myself running against the tide of people heading back into the city for a drink or back home. Tradition dictates that at the end of an Ashes series, the two teams congregate in the home dressing room to share a drink, and after chatting briefly to the handful of the Australian players that I knew reasonably well from playing with and against them, I sought out the man who had made our batters' lives hell for the past six weeks.

Mitchell Johnson was unplayable throughout that series: he finished with 37 wickets at 13.97, the most in an Ashes series since Shane Warne in 2005, and bowled unbelievably fast. International cricketers – and world-class batters like ours – become so used to facing fast bowling that the fear factor generally disappears, but it was very evidently there with Johnson. It was the best sustained fast bowling I'd ever seen: I refuse to believe that anyone has ever bowled quicker than that in the history of the game. His warm-up ball would be 91mph: he was a freak of nature. He's not a huge man, but he was so intimidating: during the Perth Test, I'd been down to the gym at the WACA for a gym session and found him there lifting some weights straight after he had bowled us out with some absolute thunderbolts. He had a big handlebar moustache and I looked at him and thought, 'This bloke is an animal.' I couldn't get my head around it: why wasn't he chilling in the dressing room after doing that?

I quickly discovered that he was nowhere near as scary off the pitch as he was on it. Mark Bawden wanted to chat to Johnson too, figuring out how he had reached such an amazing peak in his career after struggling a few years previously, and the three of us spent half an hour chatting through it. He laid it out simply: he went back to a coach that he trusted, used them as his single point of reference and tried to focus on what made him himself. He told me that he'd been singing 'Let It Go' from the film *Frozen* in his head all series: his kids loved it, and he used the song as a prompt to let any noise or baggage that threatened to distract him go, instead focusing only on his battle with the batter at the far end. I couldn't believe it: the terrifying fast bowler who had been launching 95mph rockets at my teammates all series had been singing a children's song in his head the whole time.

I was so grateful to Johnson for that conversation. I'd spent weeks taking advice on how to come back from rock bottom from people who had never experienced anything like what I was going through. Now, someone who had been there, done it, and proved that it was possible, was laying out a simple trajectory for me. It still felt a long way off, but I knew that in Richard Johnson at Middlesex, I had a coach I trusted who could help me get things right technically, and I felt like I had a road map that I could copy and paste on to my own career to make it back to the top. Without that chat, I might never have developed the same deep-rooted belief that I was going to get back to being an England regular, however hard it might be. His blueprint convinced me further that this was a technical problem, first and foremost, that I could solve with the right help from the right people: I saw the route to rediscovering my confidence not through sitting down with a psychologist and talking about it, but building it back up through practice and training well.

The trouble was, I wasn't due to get home for another month. I'd been named in the squads to play five ODIs and three T20s at the end of the tour; a few days after my chat with Johnson, I was down in Canberra preparing to play a warm-up match that would represent my first chance to bowl in a game for six weeks. At that stage of my career, I wasn't a big believer in using videos to watch myself bowl. I tried to be more of a 'feel' bowler, because I thought that using videos would overcomplicate things – much as it must seem unfathomable that I could overcomplicate things any more than I already was. But as we trained ahead of our match against the Prime Minister's XI, one of our backroom staff filmed me from all angles as I bowled to Ian Bell in the nets.

I bowled fine: I was still a long way from my best, but I wasn't spraying the ball all over the place as I had been at times on the trip. I found bowling with a white ball simpler, because my game plan tended to be much more straightforward: I just had to bowl slightly short of a good length, over the top of middle and off stump. I still have some footage of me beating Bell's outside edge in that training session, but the side-on angle shocked me. Just like the picture from Alice Springs that had rattled me earlier in the tour, it highlighted how short and rushed everything was in my action: there was no flow or whip about the way that I bowled, which I traced back to my shortened run-up. I looked at that footage and thought, 'Fuck. This shouldn't be happening. This isn't right.' I'd done all this work on trying to use my levers over the course of the trip, but it wasn't translating into my bowling at all. Even after the hope that my chat with Johnson had offered me, it felt like yet another low ebb in a tour filled with them.

# 8

# The Road Back

The evening before we were due to play the Australian Prime Minister's XI in Canberra in January 2014, the England team were hosted at Parliament House for a reception. It was there that Ashley Giles, our one-day coach, came up to me and took me to one side. He told me that I wasn't going to play the warm-up match the following day, which was a relief in itself, and then laid things out pretty clearly to me. He hadn't been around during the Test series and was so taken aback by the state that my bowling action was in when he arrived ahead of the ODIs that he realised I wasn't going to be much use to him for the next four weeks. 'We're going to send you home,' he told me, and a wave of relief took over my body.

It was, Gilo said, the kindest thing to do. He told me that I wasn't in a fit state to be playing international cricket, that I'd benefit from the break and that he saw me as an important part of the future of the team – all of the right things for someone to say in that situation. We'd had our disagreements in the past, but I enjoyed playing for him. He was a strong character – stubborn, just like I could be – and wasn't shy of telling you what he thought. He would always try to get ahead of any given situation before it got bigger than it needed to be, and this was no different: him sending me home amounted to him trying to get ahead of the situation. It was the right decision. He was absolutely spot on: I wasn't ready to bowl in international cricket, and there was no way that was going to change if I had stayed in Australia and gone through the same routine of daily torture in the nets.

But the way that it played out in the media was horrendous. I had tried to keep myself away from the press as much as possible on that tour: I saw reasonably early on that people were writing about the fact I was bowling by myself in the nets, and tried to disassociate from it completely. It wasn't helpful for me to be reading it, so I just did my best to ignore it. But it was easier said than done: Twitter was the main social media platform at the time, and if someone tagged me into something, the chances were that I'd end up seeing it. It didn't register with me that Gilo would have to front up and speak about the decision to send me home, and there was no discussion about how it might be communicated. I didn't know anything about the short statement that the ECB released until it was out in the world. *'England fast bowler Steven Finn will miss the remainder of the limited-overs series against Australia. The 24-year-old will return to the UK to continue working on technical aspects of his game.'*

Gilo fielded all sorts of questions about me at a press conference, but there was one sentence that every outlet latched on to: 'Steven is not selectable at the moment.' It was fundamentally true – I couldn't have played international cricket at that point in time – and Gilo, true to form, was being blunt and honest when he said it. If only he had known just how much it would stick in people's memories, and the impact that it would have on me. I was on the back page of *The Times* newspaper, with the headline: 'FINN DOWN AND OUT – "UNSELECTABLE" BOWLER SENT HOME FROM ENGLAND TOUR'. I hated the phrase, and the connotations of failure that it carried with it. I knew for a fact, straight away, that it would follow me around forever. I felt like I was getting battered from all angles, both inside my own head and outside it. I felt ashamed.

As I see it, the ECB stuffed me with their transparency. They could so easily have invented a muscle strain – telling people that I'd hurt my hamstring, or my quad – and said that I wouldn't be fit to play a part in the rest of the series. Instead, they hung me out to dry and left me completely vulnerable. For a couple of days, I was like a human dartboard: people could – and did – say whatever they wanted about me, whether it was true or not. It would play out very differently now: the England team's head of media and communications would send me a draft of the statement they were planning to release, and would give me the opportunity to amend it as I saw fit. Whether or not they'd play along with pretending I had a niggle, there would certainly be more vagaries around it. Instead, everyone was told loud and clear that I was going home because I wasn't in a fit state to play cricket for England.

There was one article that rubbed me up the wrong way more than any other. David Lloyd – aka 'Bumble' – was one of Sky Sports's most prominent commentators and was also the president of the Professional Cricketers' Association, the players' union, at the time. *'I'm amazed it has taken England this long to send Steven Finn home. From what I've been hearing, he should have gone back during the Test series,'* he wrote in his blog on Sky's website. *'My information (and it is second-hand) is that he's got the bowling "yips" and can't get the ball from one end to the other.'* He wrote that he'd been chatting about me *'over a curry'* with Nasser Hussain, and that he was *'very sceptical'* that my bowling action would click again – *'for Middlesex or England'*. I felt it was irresponsible, lazy and disrespectful to use that language about a young sportsman, let alone when he was president of the PCA, whose role was to look out for players. It hurt me so much, and irritated me: I thought it was just clickbait but people latched on to it because of where it had come from. When I started broadcasting, much later in my career, I vowed never to be lazy with the way I described things or to use throwaway comments without context when I was critical of someone, because I remembered how much those words affected me.

Just before I headed home, the ECB arranged for me to do an interview with their in-house channels to get my side of the story across, and to try to cool the flames that were raging out of control. It is a tough watch, even years later. I looked exhausted in it, after the hell I had put myself through physically and mentally to try and make myself feel right. '*At times, it has felt like I've been banging my head against the brick wall trying to make it right*,' I said. '*I'm nowhere near as far away as some people have been suggesting in the press: it's quite an uninformed view from people who haven't seen me bowl much*,' I said, trying to fire back at some of what I'd read or been sent. '*I've done a lot of bowling away from people's eyes and I feel I'm not far away from it clicking – but I've had two and a half months of feeling like that.*' It was as close as I came to publicly admitting what was going on – but my real emotions were the ones that poured out in the letter I wrote to myself on the flight home.

My first port of call when I got back home was to escape. I went down to Lympstone in Devon for two weeks with my partner at the time to stay with her parents, and barely looked at my phone. We went for long winter walks with the dog, enjoyed being in the countryside, and I tried to switch myself off from the bubble that England cricket can become. It might not sound like a long time after everything I'd been through in Australia, but that two-week period felt like an age to me. My trip to Fiji the year before was the only time since my Test debut that I'd taken that long a break from bowling, so switching off completely from cricket felt like a huge decision, and a huge change. It was a rare chance to just be Steven, rather than England cricketer Steven Finn: there were no longer twenty journalists watching me bowl, or thirty people in the dressing room that I had to reassure that I was OK. It did me a lot of good. By the end of it, I was itching to get back to Lord's and to get back bowling: I had a burning desire to get back and get to work to try to sort things out for good. There was never a question in my mind as to whether I was going to come through the other side of it.

At the end of the month, I sat down for a meeting at Lord's in the Writing Room – a beautiful old room which, along with the Bowlers Bar, is my favourite in the Pavilion – with Andy Flower, Angus Fraser and Richard Johnson. It must have been one of the final meetings that Flower had before he stepped down as England coach, which proved to me that for all his hard exterior, he cared deeply about my future as a cricketer. It was the moment that I reconnected with cricket after my time away, and the focus was all forward-facing. There had been lots of speculation and conjecture in the media about my Middlesex coaches butting heads with England and the ECB, but the fundamental truth was that they all wanted the same thing: to help me fulfil the potential that I had shown throughout the first few years of my international career.

There was no finger-pointing, or attribution of blame as to how I had got into such a mess by the time I left Australia. Instead, we sat down as a group and asked, 'What happens next?' Everyone knew that things had gone badly, and the question was how I could get back not only to being an

England cricketer again, but to being the bowler that I still believed I could be. I knew that it would be a long road back – I had abandoned any hope of going on the one-day tour to the West Indies, or to Bangladesh for the World T20 that followed – but it wasn't like I had completely given up on the idea that I could bowl quick, or that I didn't think I'd ever be a good bowler again. I valued the fact that I was there in the room: I had always bristled at the thought of people sitting around a table discussing what was best for me, because of that sense of control that I cherished and the responsibility that I took for my own career. As a four, we had really constructive, detailed conversations and debates about what I looked like at my best, and the little hoops that I would need to jump through in order to get back to that level.

We decided that Jono and I would go away and work on the mechanics of my bowling together. We looked at the side-on videos from the nets in Canberra, and that horrible still photo of my bent arm in Alice Springs, and devised drills that would enable me to feel like I was using my long levers again. We'd always had a good relationship – first as teammates, and then with him as Middlesex's bowling coach – but this was the first time that we'd done technical work together for a prolonged period of time. I had spent so much time away with England that he was always cautious not to intervene any more than he needed to. I was still vulnerable after what I'd been through, but Jono and Gus were the people who could put me in a safe place when it came to bowling. After spending so much time feeling like I was being watched in Australia, I decided that I wanted everything to be behind closed doors.

I'd never lived in London before, but decided to rent a place in St John's Wood for a year. It was on Hamilton Terrace, barely a stone's throw from Lord's, and meant that I could walk into the ground first thing in the morning. From early February, I'd be in at the crack of dawn, as soon as the indoor school opened, and Jono would do a session with me before staying on for Middlesex's pre-season training. I wanted to be in early, before any of my teammates could see me: I was so self-conscious, and embarrassed that I had to start from scratch. But we worked on the right stuff: we decided exactly what we would do, and stuck to it. At long last, I stopped looking for one golden nugget of information that would make me feel amazing as a short-term fix, and committed to the process of stripping everything back to basics. I realised that it was going to take a lot of time to teach myself how to feel like myself while bowling again.

We started at walking pace, and it was slow progress. 'It looks really natural,' Jono would tell me. 'It doesn't feel fucking natural,' I would fire back at him. I left a handful of sessions wondering if people were right about me all along. What if I never made it back? What if my England career was already over? But I'd always manage to snap out of it: my stubbornness took over, and we were working so diligently that the next session was never far away. After a couple of weeks, we moved back to jogging, and then finally to a full run-up indoors. It must have looked bizarre: Jono realised that I needed to drill my long run-up, rather than adjusting to a short one in the nets, which meant running most of the length of the Lord's indoor school and bowling the ball into the back net five yards away. The point was to focus on the sting off my fingertips, and the feeling of being paused at the top of my bound – all the little things that allowed me to reconnect with what had made me the bowler I was. It also meant a total focus on the process, rather than the outcome: I couldn't fixate on where the ball had landed, and dwell on the consequences of that. The only thing that mattered was the feeling of creating loads of energy and the ball stinging off the end of my fingertips. It really simplified my focus and we gradually built things back up for five days a week over a six-week period, and I slowly but surely started to feel like myself again.

We were naughty, too. I still had my ECB contract, which meant I was meant to give them details of every single time that I bowled so that they could manage my workload. But I decided I wanted to push myself hard, because I was making progress and my brain was wired towards hard work. I knew that was the style of training that I responded to, and thought that if all of my energy was channelled in the right direction, I would eventually rediscover the feelings that I used to have while I was bowling at my best. An England physio or sports scientist would probably have told me to slow down because a spreadsheet was saying not to bowl as much, but Jono and I knew that it was the right way for me to deal with things and to make progress.

There was one clip that Jono and I kept going back to, from an England Lions game against Pakistan A on the tour to the UAE in early 2010 when I first caught Flower's eye. It was a front-on clip of me charging in to have Mohammad Hafeez caught at first slip, and it was the clearest example of when my run-up and action were at their smoothest. My body had developed in the intervening four years – I'd bulked out, and put on some muscle – but the fundamentals were obvious: a bouncy, flowing run-up to the crease, a momentary delay when I got to the crease and time stood still, and then everything moving in sync as my energy came through towards the batsman. The ball moved away off the seam, and flew off

Hafeez's outside edge; I watched that footage so many times as I tried to ingrain my natural bowling action again.

I count myself very lucky that Jono was at Middlesex at the time. If I hadn't had a bowling coach that I really, genuinely trusted, I'm not sure that I'd have been able to commit completely to what I was doing, because of how scarred I was by all those different voices giving me advice and information in Australia. I had always seen Jono as a technical coach, and David Saker as a tactical one: they were the scientist and the artist respectively, which made sense for their respective roles. In county cricket, coaches have a long off-season to work on technique, and there is less scrutiny on each game; in international cricket, you are constantly in performance mode, and under pressure to perform. Jono poured a lot of time and energy into helping to build me back up, and I'm unbelievably grateful to him for it. My relationship with Gus changed slightly around that time: he became part of the England selection panel, while still working for Middlesex as director of cricket, which inevitably altered the dynamics. I'm sure I became a little bit more guarded with him as a result of it, even if he was still a trusted ally and a confidant.

I was a bag of nerves when I went out in the middle to bowl in a match situation for the first time. I'd been anxious enough bowling to my Middlesex teammates in the nets after spending so long working on my own with Jono, gradually working my way back up to full speed, but my mind was filled with doubt as we approached our first pre-season friendlies at the end of March 2014. We played Surrey in a very low-key warm-up match at Merchant Taylors' School, but my second friendly back – against Somerset at Taunton – is the one that sticks in my mind. I doubted whether everything I had worked on in practice was going to stay in place when I went into a competitive environment: sometimes, what you do in training just doesn't seem to translate into bowling well in the middle. Your mind can transport you back to the bad times and you can revert to those bad habits when under more pressure. That's why we were so meticulous about my path back to competitive cricket.

My focus was on trying to take baby steps: I had a deep-rooted fear of old bad habits creeping back in, and mental scars being reopened. It had been nearly four months since my last competitive bowl, down in Alice Springs. That might not sound like much, but it was by far the longest gap between cricket matches I'd had since becoming an England player. Taunton was renowned for being an incredibly flat pitch – a bowler's graveyard – and even though there was hardly anyone in the ground, I felt the same pressure as I used to in international cricket. I bowled 21 overs in that friendly, dismissing two former England players in Marcus Trescothick and Nick Compton, and came away feeling pretty good about it. I wasn't perfect – my body was still a bit tangled – but it was an important box ticked.

I ticked another in early April, playing in Middlesex's first game of the County Championship season, and holding my own down at Hove against Sussex. I was bowling first change, even though I had always loved opening the bowling. It was definitely the right thing at the time, because I was trying to embed all this technical work while playing competitive cricket at the same time; removing the responsibility of being the attack leader and taking the new ball helped to relieve the pressure on me, which already felt quite substantial. I struggled in my first spell with the added adrenaline of playing in a game with consequence, but finished that match with figures of 6 for 80 – including my England teammate Matt Prior, who helped me off his hip straight down to the fielder at long leg. I took nine in the match against Nottinghamshire at Lord's soon after, and while I certainly wasn't bowling like I had done two years previously, I started to feel more like my old self. The technical tweaks were working, and I was starting to master again the skill that once felt so natural to me: playing around with my angles on the crease, finally starting to get in battles with the batter at the other end as opposed to the one going on inside my head.

I had a great battle with Joe Root when we played Yorkshire. Rooty had been dropped for the final Test of the 2013/14 Ashes, and this was the first – and only – time he experienced trying to prove himself again in county cricket to force his way back into the team. We had become good mates: he broke his thumb on the one-day tour to the West Indies that followed the Ashes, and I have a vivid memory of him rocking up to my house-warming in St John's Wood – which I had in a pub around the corner because I didn't trust all my reprobate friends to not make a mess of my new flat – with a big bandage on it. A few weeks later, we were having a proper battle with one another: he was convinced the umpire had made a terrible decision to give him out lbw to me in the first innings, and we had a good back and forth during the second: we were chirping at each other after he top-edged my bouncer for six, and I felt a lot of satisfaction when I trapped him lbw for the second time in the match. He still insists to this day that neither were out. Typical batsman.

I took four wickets in each innings of that game, and we pulled off a miracle win: Chris Rogers played a ridiculous innings, hitting 241 not out as we chased down a huge fourth innings target, which must be the best I've seen someone play in a Middlesex shirt. Rogers had been recalled to the

Australia side for the 2013 Ashes and had been part of the side that thrashed us 5–0 the previous winter, and he was a great guy who deserved his success. He had joined as our overseas player in 2011, took over as captain soon after, and was a friend first and foremost, rather than an Ashes rival. We socialised a lot together, and he had seen me retreat into myself the previous summer when things weren't going well. I always felt as though he was supportive of me and was perfect for the Middlesex team at the time, a strong character who led the dressing room. It was a common experience for me with the Australians I played with at Middlesex: David Warner, Phil Hughes, Adam Voges and George Bailey – along with Rogers – were all competitive guys who could get stuck in during the confrontation of an Ashes battle, but I always enjoyed their company as teammates.

I picked up wickets throughout those first few games back playing and was one of the leading wicket-takers in the Championship. I felt like I was ahead of the game: I was just happy to be back bowling and playing competitive cricket again, so the fact I was taking regular wickets was an added bonus. I knew that I wasn't totally sorted: I was still having to focus hard on making sure that my body was where I wanted it to be at each stage of my bowling action, but the path back was suddenly much clearer than it had been four or five months previously in Australia. I certainly didn't feel as though I'd be close to playing Test cricket when the first squad of the summer was named: Peter Moores had replaced Flower as head coach, and there was a new look and feel to the side with no Jonathan Trott, Kevin Pietersen or Graeme Swann. I wasn't in the slightest bit surprised to miss out, with Liam Plunkett and Chris Jordan both ahead of me, but my performances for

Middlesex helped reinforce the sense that all the work Jono and I had done together was building me back up.

It would have been easy for me to shy away, or to take a much slower approach to my comeback, but I was still young, stubborn and headstrong. I was an England-contracted player, too, and figured that hiding away in the shadows would only make people talk more than they already were. That was the last thing I wanted. Middlesex were great with me, all through the summer. I wasn't technically their player – the ECB became my primary employers as soon as I was awarded my first central contract in 2010 – but they invested so much time and effort into helping me get back to being myself. The rest of the squad got around me as players, with both Rogers and Eoin Morgan being incredibly supportive as our Championship and white-ball captains respectively, and Jono and Gus both played big roles too. They would all have known how tough that Australia tour had been for me, and wanted to help me put it behind me and move forward.

Sam Robson was my closest mate, and it remains a big regret that we never played for England together. He had been churning out the runs for Middlesex for a number of years, and got his chance to open the batting during that 2014 summer. We had a T20 training session at Merchant Taylors' School on the morning of his debut, but everyone was desperate to get to Lord's straight after to watch Sam playing for England for the first time. We started early, finished early, dashed back into London and got to Lord's just after the start of play at 11 a.m. Sri Lanka had chosen to bowl first, and by the time we got into our seats in the Mound Stand, where his friends and family were sitting, he had nicked off! It would have been amazing to play Test cricket with him, but clearly it wasn't meant to be.

I kept taking wickets as the summer wore on, removing

the battle from inside my head and immersing myself in playing competitively, and in early August, I was recalled to the England squad for the last two Tests against India when Plunkett went down injured. I had an imaginary ladder in my head, with bowling in a Test match right at the top, and getting my first call-up into the squad was like climbing another rung. I didn't ever sense that I had a realistic chance of playing against India, but I was desperate to get back into the England environment. Peter Moores was helpful through the summer with his communication, letting me know that he wanted me back into the international fold once I was ready, and adding me to that squad allowed me to reintegrate slowly rather than being thrown back in at the deep end.

Driving up to Manchester, I questioned in my own head whether I was ready to play international cricket again, and whether I deserved to be there. But I had taken a lot of wickets in the summer and felt like I had jumped through every hoop that had been asked of me. When I reached Old Trafford, I was handed a grey plastic bag with 'FINN' written on it – think of being given a parcel by a delivery driver – which was how players received their training and match kit. It was the sort of moment that I had started to take for granted when I was part of every single England squad across all formats, but after seven months on the sidelines, it gave me a real buzz. 'Fuck, I've missed this,' I thought. Even the build-up to a game felt different: for all that county cricket serves an important purpose, seeing the photographers and TV cameras around the ground on training days was a reminder that this would be another real step-up in intensity.

I missed out on selection, unsurprisingly, for the final two India Tests, but was picked for the ODI series that followed – another box checked, another rung climbed on the ladder.

I knew that despite the technical work I had undergone, I could still bowl 90-odd miles per hour: that was an unusual skill in English cricket, and this was proof that the England management were aware of that too. It was at Trent Bridge – the scene of my most recent Test match, and that punishing weights session after our epic Ashes win the previous summer – that I made my return to international cricket. We were heavily beaten, but I held my own with the ball and celebrated with a big fist pump after having Ajinkya Rahane, the stylish Indian opener, caught behind by one of my closest friends, Jos Buttler. After our debrief, everyone else filtered out of the dressing room to leave just me and Moores in the dressing room. I sat there for a moment, took a deep breath and felt an overwhelming sense of relief, reflecting on how far away from this I felt just six months ago. After everything I had been through, I had played international cricket again, got a good player out, and proved – to myself more than anyone – that I was resilient enough to overcome the huge hurdle that I had faced. England simply didn't consider one-day internationals to be as important as Test cricket at that time, so it didn't quite feel like I had climbed Everest. But at least I had reached base camp, and I had completed a long journey back in a short space of time.

I was still a closed book for most of that summer. Later in the ODI series, we were at Headingley when David Young, a psychologist I knew from Middlesex who was working with the England team, came up to me and asked if I wanted to talk about anxiety. I had been through a lot in the past eighteen months or so, and he would not have been blind to the fact that it had taken a toll on my mental wellbeing, but I had no interest in opening up to him. 'No, I do not want to talk about it,' I told him bluntly, refusing to acknowledge the idea that there was anything to talk about. I didn't want to let anyone – even my teammates – in on the fact that I felt vulnerable. My perception at the time was that I wanted – and needed – to be a macho, tough fast bowler, and that any sense of vulnerability would count against me. With hindsight, I don't think it would have done, but I felt like after all the hard work I had done on my bowling to reach the point I had, the last thing I needed was to start opening up about all of the shit I had been through in Australia – even if in the long run it would have helped me.

I still don't know what the right answer was. I turned twenty-five that year, and was the product of the dressing-room environment that I had been part of throughout my adult life. It wasn't the done thing to admit any vulnerability at all. I was so stubbornly focused on coming back that I insisted to everyone – including myself – that the only issues I had faced in Australia were technical problems with my bowling action. Yes, my confidence had taken a beating, but my logic was that this was as a result of my technical problems; once I sorted those out, I would feel invincible again. It made me laser-focused on getting my action sorted, and that in turn helped me come back as quickly as I did. If I had sought professional help and started to address some of my deeper-lying problems with confidence and anxiety at that time, I don't think I'd have been able to return to international cricket seven months after flying home from Australia. It would only have set me back even further. Does that mean I did the right thing? The honest answer is that I'm not sure. I am incredibly proud that I showed the resilience I did during that time, even if the longer-term implications were negative – and I recognise the contradictions within those feelings.

At the end of the summer, I was given another big confidence boost. I'd been nervous for a while about losing my

England central contract: at the time, the contract system was heavily weighted towards Test cricket, and I'd not played a Test match since the previous summer. I'd negotiated a decent 'shadow' contract with Middlesex, which meant the financial implications weren't as worrying as they might have been, but I felt as though dropping off the contract list would be a signal that my standing had fallen. There was an aspirational element to it, too: there were only twelve names on that list, and I was desperate to be one of them. I was incredibly anxious as I sat on a stool in a corridor at Loughborough waiting for my appraisal, as though I was waiting to be told off by the headmaster at school.

I was convinced when Paul Downton, England's managing director, called me into the room that it would be bad news, and I felt a huge sense of reassurance wash over me when he told me my contract would be renewed. I had gone down a salary band, but he said that the ECB valued my contributions to the team highly, wanted to support me, and saw me playing a big role in helping England achieve their upcoming targets: competing well at the 50-over World Cup in early 2015, and regaining the Ashes on home soil in the summer. It was exactly what I needed to hear. I felt like I was back where I belonged.

# 9

# Australia Again

England's 2014/15 winter was all geared around the 2015 World Cup in Australia and New Zealand, a tournament I had always wanted to play in. We had a full schedule of one-day cricket, which was enabled by the ECB and Cricket Australia shifting the Ashes forward the previous winter, and we had a long preparation period that should have allowed us to arrive at the World Cup feeling like we were ready to hit the ground running. Instead, it was chaos: Alastair Cook was dropped and removed as captain after our 5–2 series loss in Sri Lanka, and Eoin Morgan took over so close to the start of the World Cup that he had no opportunity to put his stamp on the team. It was a hospital pass for Eoin, with months of planning ripped up and put in the bin just before we left for Australia. It was a familiar story for England at World Cups, and one which reflected the fact that one-day cricket was always an afterthought to Test matches.

It was in Sri Lanka that we heard the news that turned the sport upside down: Phil Hughes, my old Middlesex teammate and Ashes rival, had been struck on the top of his neck by a bouncer in a Sheffield Shield game and passed away after two nights in hospital. News filtered through to us that he'd been hit, and it was hard to compute when we saw on

Twitter that he'd been pronounced dead. I was asked to do the England press conference later that day, and struggled to hold it together: I was preparing a few answers in my head, since I knew I'd be asked about Hughesy, and bawled my eyes out in front of the team's media manager. I couldn't really comprehend what had happened: he was twenty-five, the same age as me, and we had always made a point of keeping up with one another after his time at Middlesex in 2009. It just didn't seem real to me. We swapped shirts at the end of the 2010/11 Ashes, after the Sydney Test, and it is a big regret that I never managed to get him to sign it; we'd mentioned it a few times over the years, but always assumed there would be another opportunity.

It definitely changed my mindset for a while, too. It made me nervous to bowl a short ball in practice: what if I hit someone, and they never recovered? Much as I saw Hughesy's death as a freak incident, it was a stark reminder that my job was to bowl a cricket ball at 90mph at someone: there was always a chance that I would inadvertently inflict some serious damage. We really struggled to get Mahela Jayawardene out in that one-day series, and we hatched a plan to go around the wicket and test him out against the short ball. I stood at the top of my mark and thought, 'Fucking hell. Do I really want to do this?' It made bowling – and sport – feel very different for a while.

I had some trepidation about heading back to Australia after my experience there the previous winter, but I felt like I was hitting my straps and saw the World Cup as another opportunity to prove myself against the best. It was a sign of how far my mindset had come along in a year because I was excited about trying to help win games of cricket in that environment. It was a big tournament in itself, of course, but I also saw it as another step towards my ultimate goal of getting back into the

Test team ahead of the 2015 Ashes. I loved playing one-day cricket – and my ODI record was better than my Test one – but I viewed it as a stepping stone; that was probably symptomatic of where white-ball cricket sat in the pecking order for the ECB at the time.

When you have done technical work on your action, the challenge is to make sure your focus is on the battle with the batsman at the other end of the pitch, rather than a battle with yourself. After spending the summer gradually building back up, taking wickets and slowly growing in confidence, my focus was at the far end. I went into that tournament naive as to how quickly one-day cricket had changed: other teams were scoring far quicker than before, and England's template of trying to scrap our way past 250 by keeping wickets in hand had become outdated. I realised we weren't favourites for the World Cup, but genuinely felt as though we had a squad that could compete well enough in high-pressure moments that we would go deep into the tournament.

We played a tri-series against Australia and India in the build-up, which was a chance to stake my claim for inclusion at the start of the World Cup. It started in Sydney, where I received a typically friendly reception from the fans. During Australia's run chase, I lost my footing as my back foot landed at the crease, slipped and fell. I was fine, but as I picked myself up and walked back to the top of my mark a little embarrassed. As I headed back to fine leg at the end of my over, I heard a guy in the Bill O'Reilly Stand at the SCG starting a chant: 'Give me an "F"! Give me an "I"! Give me an "N"! Give me an "N"! What does it spell?' The whole stand yelled back at him: 'SHIT!' Welcome back to Australia.

Next up was Brisbane. I was conscious that I'd flown home from there the previous year, and was back staying in the same hotel, but I was so bloody-minded and stubborn that I was determined to kick on and look forward. Chris Jordan was ahead of me in the pecking order at the start of that tour, but missed our game against India at the Gabba with an illness and I seized the opportunity of a last-minute call-up. I had only played there once before and had good memories of that six-wicket haul in the 2010/11 Ashes, even if I had been self-critical at the time. The pitch suited me to perfection: it has the type of steepling bounce from a full length that, if you're in form, makes you so excited to bowl on. I bowled as well as I had since coming back into the England team: I took 5 for 33, finding that bounce to nick off Virat Kohli, and knew that I had a great chance of playing when the World Cup started a couple of weeks later. The worries and stress of the thoughts inside my own head of last year felt so far away. I was just thinking about how to get people out.

The tournament started for us at the MCG, and after missing out on the Ashes Test there four years previously, I was excited to get to play there for the first time. There was an incredible atmosphere, with 93,000 people there, and the nerves that I felt were positive ones: I could hear the buzz as I sat in the vast Australian Rules football dressing room. I was full of adrenaline before playing in front of such a big crowd, rather than anxious about the prospect of anything going wrong. Anxiety, at varying levels, is part and parcel of being an international sportsperson. It's what makes the game so exciting. Can you use that nervous energy and turn it into a feeling that helps you perform? It made me realise that the anxiety I'd been feeling twelve months ago was completely different: it had been all-consuming and affected every part of my life, not just around cricket.

We were thrashed, losing by 111 runs, and the ease with

which Australia reached 342 was a wake-up call: that sort of total was beyond our wildest dreams as a side, and we quickly realised that we were on the back foot. Everyone burst out laughing at the end of their innings, when I took one of the all-time great hat-tricks: Brad Haddin, caught at deep third man; Glenn Maxwell, caught at long-off; and Mitchell Johnson, caught at mid-off. I'd always dreamed of taking a hat-trick for my country; I can't say I had pictured it as three men caught slogging off the final three balls of the innings to finish with 5 for 71 in 10 overs.

I came away from our second game, against New Zealand in Wellington, in a state of total shell shock. I was decent mates with their fast bowler Tim Southee, and had a good chat with him before the game. He was relaxed as always, but it seemed to me that New Zealand clearly saw that World Cup as a real opportunity to make their mark on a global stage, playing on home soil and with a really strong team, and the crowd was louder than I'd ever heard before in New Zealand. I had memories of playing domestic cricket there and touring with England and it's an amazing place. The people are hospitable and friendly, the food and wine is incredible and it has always been one of my favourite places to tour. But this crowd was hostile: you could sense they wanted some England heads on stakes. They got them, and Southee ran through us: it was embarrassing enough being part of a team that was bowled out for 123, but the real humiliation was still to come. Our innings was so short that we had to go out and bowl before the dinner break: in that scenario, most teams would just knock the ball around until the interval, and then look to crack on with winning the game after the break.

Not New Zealand. Brendon McCullum and Martin Guptill came out as though they were trying to hit every single ball that we bowled for four or six, and had already scored 37 by the time I was brought into the attack for the fourth over. McCullum charged at my first ball and launched me over extra cover for six, but I wasn't panicking: I'd had some success against him before, and thought I would keep things simple, look to hit the splice of his bat, and wait for him to skew one up in the air as he seemed to have done before off my bowling. But he just kept on coming: my second and fourth balls went for four, and my fifth disappeared back over my head for another six. Bloody hell. In my second over, the only plan I could come up with under pressure was to try and bowl faster and faster, but the quicker I bowled, the further I went: McCullum was an unbelievably destructive player on his day, and cracked me for four successive sixes. My figures were eye-watering: 0 for 49 in two overs. Time passed so quickly that day. I rushed through my overs and felt like I didn't give myself time to think in between balls, clouding my mind even further. It's part of what makes it so intimidating to bowl at batters playing so aggressively.

When we walked off for the dinner break after nine overs, New Zealand needed 12 to win. The dressing room was completely silent, and I stared at the floor for forty minutes with my head down. Peter Moores, our head coach, was so desperate to keep our spirits up that he tapped me on the knee and said, 'Your pace was good.' I thought, 'Mate, I've just gone for 49 in two overs!' I wanted a hole to open up so that I could jump into it and never come out. I had arranged to see Guptill and his wife, the broadcaster Laura McGoldrick, for a drink after the game, and we'd planned to meet up regardless of the result: it was only cricket, after all. Needless to say, after the manner of that defeat, I was pretty quick to call it off. I spent that evening sat in my room with the TV off, staring at the ceiling.

It might sound counter-intuitive, but I managed to write that day off in my own head pretty quickly: it was so bad, and such an extreme set of circumstances, that I considered it as a one-off. It wasn't like I'd gone for 100 off 10 overs – though if we'd have bowled first and I had kept on conceding runs at that rate, I could have gone for 245. It was so quick and so brutal that the whole thing felt almost surreal. I couldn't quite believe that the whole thing had happened: it felt like an out-of-body experience. I know it is hard to believe, given my bad memories in that part of the world and the fact that I'd just bowled the two most expensive overs of my career, but it genuinely didn't dent my confidence. I didn't have much time to dwell on it, either: three days later, I took 3 for 26 in nine overs in our next game against Scotland. That felt like proof that the New Zealand game was a total freak occurrence, and an outlier, rather than an indication that I was doing anything wrong.

We were thrashed again by Sri Lanka in Wellington, and I was dropped for the defeat to Bangladesh that confirmed our elimination before we had even reached the quarter-finals. I never enjoyed being left out, but I didn't take this one too badly: I knew that Chris Jordan had started the trip ahead of me in the pecking order, and wasn't surprised that we were looking to make changes once we had started losing. I'd been whacked around in a couple of games, but didn't come back from the World Cup feeling like it had been a huge setback to me personally. I was our leading wicket-taker in the tri-series with Australia and India beforehand, and despite missing our last two games, I finished the World Cup as our leading wicket-taker, too. It wasn't much of an achievement given how badly our tournament had gone, but none of my peers had outperformed me. Instead, it was just confirmation that England's white-ball cricket had fallen a long way behind the rest of the world: there were some heated exchanges during a tetchy meeting at our team hotel in Sydney before we flew home, but we all knew that we were miles off where we needed to be to compete at major tournaments.

I spent the week sulking after finding out that I wasn't going to be picked for the Test series in the West Indies that came straight after the World Cup, but it turned out to be the best thing that could have happened to me. I felt like I deserved to be in the squad as I felt like I'd made big strides even given the challenges of the winter, and had a burning desire to play Test cricket again. I wanted to prove myself at that level after so long away and thought I had proved myself with a strong Championship season for Middlesex, but the selectors saw it otherwise.

I grew particularly frustrated with hearing people tell me I'd lost pace, when I knew that I hadn't: I might not have been touching 95mph any more, but I was still consistently operating in the high 80s and peaking in the low 90s, which had been the case for 90 per cent of my international career. But it forced me to take a step back before the start of the 2015 summer, and that breathing space meant I had time to work on the next aspect of my bowling. I felt confident in my bowling again, and had sorted my arms out during all of the remedial work that I'd done with Richard Johnson the previous year: that was all locked in and had reached a good place. The next step was to sort my feet out: they were still crossing over when I ran to the crease, and I had enough time at home to focus properly on my stride pattern.

I had some lingering anxieties about getting external help

after listening to so many different voices in Australia, but made sure that everything was done in conjunction with Jono. Kevin Shine at the ECB introduced me to Raph Brandon, their new head of science and medicine, who had worked with Christine Ohuruogu, the 400 metres world and Olympics champion, as her running coach, and we set about sorting my feet out. He was a matter-of-fact coach who took one look at my run-up and told me, bluntly, that it was no good. 'You can't run like that.' But he invested a lot of time and effort into putting it right. It's strange: my natural running style was fluent and linear, but my gait changed as soon as you put a ball in my hand. I was losing energy in my run-up, but the corrective work I did meant that I was flowing towards the crease and moving forward throughout, rather than from side to side.

Anyone who saw me doing those drills must have thought I was crackers. I'd be on the Nursery Ground at Lord's, or in the indoor school at Loughborough, with a bunch of cones set out, running backwards for 60 metres with a cricket ball in my hand; there was another where I had to run sideways, pumping my knees, all designed to enable me to run more naturally when I had a cricket ball in my hand. I trusted Raph, and we worked diligently together – helped out by Andy Mitchell, the Middlesex strength and conditioning coach, who still barks those running drills at me every time I see him, even now. We used the time off after the World Cup really productively, so I felt confident heading into the 2015 season, and I continued to do those drills before every day of bowling in the early months of the summer. It also meant that I could stop worrying about knocking the bails off once and for all, because my knee was no longer jutting out as much in my delivery stride. I'd spent a long time painstakingly marking lines near the crease with a tape measure and spray paint to ensure that I was running in wide enough, but I could finally put a stop to that now that I could trust my run-up again.

It was a good example of Jono's brilliance as a coach. He realised in early 2014 that building me back up would be a gradual process, so focused on one thing at a time: we sorted my arms out, which in turn helped me build up my confidence, and didn't try to do too much with my feet until I had ingrained all the work I had already done. We would talk about it like a car getting its MOT, making sure my action was ready for the road. I was still making sure to follow the advice that Mitchell Johnson had given me in the SCG dressing rooms at the end of the 2013/14 tour: find a coach that you trust, back the system up, and have faith that all of the work that you're doing is enough. I always kept his advice at the back of my mind, because he was living proof that I could get back to the top.

I missed out on the squads for the first Test series of the home summer against New Zealand, and had the bit between my teeth. This time, I told myself, 'You are going to play Test cricket again this summer.' I felt like I was ready again, and that my bowling was back to Test standard. Instead of dragging my feet and being pissed off that I wasn't involved, I used it as motivation: being left out spurred me on, and made me even more determined that I would be part of the Ashes series later in the summer.

I loved the one-day series against New Zealand, which marked the start of a new era in England's white-ball cricket. Eoin Morgan had been backed to continue as captain after the World Cup and now had the chance to put his stamp on our side. There were lots of new faces in the squad – like Jason Roy, Sam Billings and Adil Rashid – and we had a young, exciting group of players who all loved to take the game on and play attacking cricket. Eoin told us all that he wanted his England to play with that same fearless attitude, and that players would be backed all the way: batters wouldn't be dropped for playing attacking shots and getting caught on the boundary, and bowlers were told to focus on taking wickets rather than worrying about their economy rates. James Anderson and Stuart Broad were phased out of white-ball cricket, which meant I was opening the bowling and setting the tone. I felt like a huge part of our new-look team.

It started with a bang: I was at the non-striker's end in the series opener at Edgbaston when Liam Plunkett hit the first ball he faced for six, taking us past 400 in an ODI for the first time. We knew New Zealand would come hard at us in reply, and when McCullum hit me for two consecutive fours in my first over, I had flashbacks to Wellington. But he charged down again to try and make it three in a row, missed, and I roared in celebration as the ball hit the top of off stump. It felt like a significant moment for me and for the team, putting the World Cup behind us once and for all, and I came away from Edgbaston with 4 for 35 from my seven overs. I felt great, bowled well throughout the series, and when I was picked for a pre-Ashes training camp at Desert Springs in Spain at the end of the month, I knew that my dream of a Test comeback was another step closer.

I always loved the chance to lead the bowling attack for England: it didn't happen often, but that New Zealand series was further evidence that it helped me to raise my game, as I had on the India one-day tours in the 2011/12 and 2012/13 winters. Yet I never, ever had the feeling that Jimmy and Broady were in any way blocking my path to success; in fact, it was the opposite. I'm not dumb: I knew they were both better bowlers than me. There were a couple of instances where I'd taken the new ball in Test cricket ahead of Stuart, and often had in one-day cricket, but Jimmy was a much, much better bowler than me, and they both had incredible international careers. They were a big part of my success: they both looked after me, and took me under their wings when I first came into the England set-up. From the outside in, you might look at it and think, 'Well, they were taking two out of three spots for fast bowlers,' but we wouldn't have been the team that we were without them in it. England only lost one Test series that I played in – against South Africa in 2012 – and I would never have wanted to trade my career for one where I won fifteen more Test caps but played for a mediocre side.

I knew when I was named in the squad for the first Test in Cardiff that I was unlikely to play. Mark Wood, the Durham fast bowler with an infectious personality, had burst on to the scene at the start of the summer and was the man in possession, but I was absolutely determined to make a strong impression in the nets. There had been another clear-out after the World Cup, with Peter Moores removed as head coach and replaced by the Australian Trevor Bayliss. Paul Farbrace, who had been involved for a year as assistant coach, stood in for Bayliss during New Zealand's tour and made clear that he was an advocate of an attacking style of cricket. He was relentlessly positive, which felt like a breath of fresh air: we had all grown so used to Andy Flower's precision, focus and attention to detail that it was incredibly liberating to be told how good we all were.

We had a new bowling coach too: Ottis Gibson, the former West Indies seamer whom I had played under at age-group level, had taken over from David Saker. Despite everything, I never held a grudge against Saker. I knew that he had only ever encouraged the short run-up because he thought it would help me become a better bowler, and he never would have pushed it if he'd known how damaging its knock-on effects would be. I only ever adopted it because I felt backed into a corner after kneeing the stumps, and with the law change that it prompted, not because he forced me to. I always enjoyed his company, and he was a huge part of the dressing room environment that made us successful. But after the best part of five years working with the same England bowling coach, I must admit that I was grateful to have a new set of eyes on me. That is not a slight on Saker's coaching. He was a good tactical coach who helped me to learn the art of setting batters up and exploiting their weaknesses. But Gibbo came in without any preconceptions, and helped me improve as a bowler almost immediately.

I arrived at that first nets session in Cardiff determined to show Bayliss how good I was: I would usually bowl with a relatively worn ball in training, but picked out the newest one that I could find to give me as much assistance as possible. I could sense Bayliss watching me as he lurked at the back of the nets, chewing his fingernails with his trademark wide-brim sunhat on. I thought back to Pretoria in 2009, when I trained in front of Flower for the first time but bowled with inhibitions and felt invisible to him. I wasn't going to let this opportunity slip. I charged in and bowled a hostile spell to Ian Bell, beating him repeatedly on his outside edge. I knew that Bayliss would sit up and take notice: even though I missed out on selection in Cardiff, as expected, I had made sure that he knew how dangerous a bowler I could be for his England team.

It was in that very same nets session that I had a Eureka moment when talking to Gibbo. For a decent while, I had been holding the ball wobble-seam: splitting my fingers, with the seam between them pointing towards where leg slip would be. I'd then pull down the back of the ball and it would create a wobble on the seam that meant I could control the line I was bowling and allow the ball to move laterally off the pitch, if there was any assistance. I had spent a long time building my confidence back up after that Australia tour, and found that holding the ball wobble-seam meant there was one less variable to worry about than if I had been trying to swing it. Early in that 2015 summer, I had spoken to Jono about trying to develop an outswinger, which we worked hard on, and I would occasionally bowl it for one or two balls in a spell while playing for Middlesex. I felt like I could trust my bowling action again so was determined to develop my skills, but didn't quite have the confidence to use my outswinger regularly.

I was apprehensive when I mentioned to Gibbo that I'd been working on it: in the back of my mind, I couldn't help but remember the bollocking that Flower had dished out in Auckland when I experimented with an outswinger during our 2013 Test series in New Zealand. I was reluctant to tell an England coach that I was trying to move the ball away from right-handers as a result of that ticking-off, but this was a different coach with a different attitude. Gibbo furrowed his brow and asked me, 'Why would you *not* want to move the ball? You have to move the ball to be dangerous.' I felt a weight lift from my shoulders, and used my outswinger throughout that spell to Bell in the nets.

I left the squad in Cardiff during the first Test – which we won comfortably, with Joe Root leading the way – and drove up to Merchant Taylors' School to play for Middlesex against Somerset in the Championship. Empowered by my conversation with Gibbo, I felt like all of the inhibitions that I had developed over the last two years had lifted, and decided I would commit to holding the ball seam up and swinging it away from the right-handers. I was so confident, and just thought, 'Fuck it. What have I got to lose?' One quick chat with a new bowling coach at the back of the nets had unlocked the mindset that I had spent years chasing. Everything clicked: I took 4 for 41 from 21 overs, and I felt like every single ball I bowled was a chance to take a wicket. I was moving the ball with control, bowling 86 or 87mph, and nipping the odd ball back off the seam with natural variation. After five years as an England player, I had suddenly unlocked a new skill that would make me even more dangerous.

I was gutted, but not surprised, to miss out on the Lord's Test. Playing in the Ashes at my home ground would have been special, but I could understand why the selectors stuck with the same team that had won in Cardiff. I trained hard again, trying to push my case to play a role in the final three Tests, and was doing some catching practice just before the toss on the first day when the whole summer flashed in front of my eyes. Farbrace was hitting plastic Incrediballs at me in front of the Tavern Stand, and whacked one flat and hard. It rose up at me like a flying saucer and smacked me on the end of my left index finger. I knew immediately that I was in trouble: my finger swelled up, turned purple, and felt unbelievably painful. I was sent off for a scan, which diagnosed a chip at the top of the bone.

I couldn't believe my bad luck, but was determined that a broken finger wasn't going to stop me. I begged the medical team to do everything in their power to make sure I would be able to play. Thankfully, it wasn't on my bowling hand, and because I was a number 11 batter, I felt like I could still contribute just as much despite the injury. I wore a plastic splint on the end of my finger, strapped up with plasters and bandages, and it was seriously uncomfortable batting with it on: we had to modify and reinforce my batting glove to make sure that I didn't do any further damage to it, and it took me a couple of sessions to work out how to catch without using my index finger on my left hand. But after everything I'd been through, spending two years working my way back into contention and feeling primed and ready to go for a home Ashes, there was no chance that a little chipped bone on my non-bowling hand was going to rule me out.

We were thrashed at Lord's, losing by 405 runs as Australia squared the series at 1–1. Steve Smith, who had established himself as the best young batsman in the world, scored a brilliant double century, and my old Middlesex teammate Chris Rogers hit 173. With our bowlers struggling, and Woody's ankle causing him some problems, I headed to Birmingham for the third Test feeling like I had every chance of making my comeback. In the eighteen months since coming home from Australia, I had climbed every rung on the ladder, gradually working my way back from rock bottom through sheer bloody-mindedness. Now, it was my chance to prove that I could make it all the way back to the top.

# 10

# Edgbaston Elation

I stood at the top of my mark at Edgbaston and took a deep breath. After 745 days away, I was about to bowl my first ball back in Test cricket and could feel my body fizzing with nervous energy. I had gone through my routine, bowling three practice balls to the fielder at mid-off. Steve Smith, fresh from his double hundred in Australia's series-squaring win at Lord's and number 1 in the ICC's batting rankings, stood waiting at the far end, surveying the field. I took a couple of seconds longer than I usually would to compose myself, and looked at the hard, new Dukes ball in my hand. I had a choice to make: should I bowl wobble-seam, so that I could control the line and ease my way back into Test cricket? Or should I commit to the work I had been doing on my outswinger, hold the ball seam up and try to swing it away from Smith's outside edge? Mitchell Johnson's words from the SCG changing rooms were in the back of my mind: trust that all of the work you're doing is enough. I made my decision and ran in, feeling the snap of the seam off my fingertips as I committed to the outswinger.

Smith left the ball alone outside off stump as it moved away from him, and I had done it: I was back playing Test cricket, back in the battle of an Ashes series, and back holding my own against the best players in the world. It was only one ball, but it reinforced that I could do this. I felt a weight lifted off my shoulders. Conditions at Edgbaston that morning were perfect for bowling: gloomy skies, slightly muggy and plenty of life in the pitch for our seamers to exploit. Jimmy Anderson bowled brilliantly with the new ball, trapping David Warner lbw and beating the bat several times, and I was raring to go in the field. I could feel the nervous energy running through my body. It was good captaincy from Alastair Cook to bring me into the attack after only seven overs, recognising that I wanted to get into the battle as quickly as possible to settle those nerves. Smith defended my second ball into the off side, then punched my third towards mid-on. Three balls bowled, no runs conceded. Most importantly, I felt free. You're acutely aware of the crowd when you're out in the middle but you have tunnel vision. You're solely focused on the twenty-two yards of the pitch, and your mind blanks out the noise around you. Finding this headspace is imperative for you to concentrate, and to stay calm – and I was there.

The fourth ball swung away late, beating the outside edge as Smith shuffled across his stumps and looked to drive me through the off side. I was on top, and reinforced to myself that I had made the right choice in holding the ball seam up and trying to swing it away from Smith's outside edge. We'd had endless discussions about how to bowl to Smith, which could easily have clouded my mind. He was a unique player, standing a long way across his stumps and whipping everything through midwicket with a strong bottom hand, which meant that people threw all sorts of unusual plans out there. Should we come wide on the crease, looking to bowl very wide outside his off stump? It was even suggested we could go around the wicket to him and angle every ball across him? But I resisted the temptation to get funky as it was the start of the innings and told myself to keep trying to bowl my best ball: rather than getting drawn into his potential weaknesses, I wanted to back my own strengths, and to be the best version of myself. I knew that my best ball would trouble the best players in the world, and my fourth ball only reinforced that.

My fifth ball brought me back to earth: I bowled a floaty half-volley, which Smith leaned into and crunched through cover for four. Shit. Maybe I wasn't in quite as much control as I thought I was. Doubts crept in. Was I still good enough? Did I deserve to be here? I turned and walked back to my mark and told myself, 'You've got this.' I just had to trust my process, trust the work I had been doing, and believe that my best ball was good enough. I had bowled well in county cricket, and had dismissed top players like Virat Kohli in ODIs. I'd jumped through every hoop I had put there for myself to get back to this point. This was a different level, but the fundamentals were the same: if I could bowl my outswinger at decent pace and land it in a good area, around fourth stump, it was good enough to get anyone in the world out – even Smith. I just needed to drag my length back a touch. I ran in hard, solely focused on that. I angled the ball in towards Smith's off stump, hit that perfect length and found just enough movement away for the ball to kiss his outside edge. Time seemed to slow down as the ball skewed off his bat, veering past Jos Buttler's right glove and dropping down towards Cooky's feet as he stood waiting at first slip. He crouched down to his left, keeping his hands low, and clung on to the ball. Smith, caught Cook, bowled Finn, 7.

I was back. I celebrated like I had never done before, jumping around with my fist clenched and roaring as my teammates mobbed me. All the shit I'd been through over the last two years, all the tears that I'd cried in Australia, and all the hard work that I'd put myself through came spilling out of me. I never planned my celebrations – I would usually wag my finger, or wheel away Alan Shearer-style with my arm in the air – but this was a pure release of the pent-up emotions that I'd left bubbling away inside of me. It was vindication for every hour of training I had done since getting home from Australia at the start of 2014, and a 'fuck you' to everyone who had written me off. The fact it was Smith added to it. I hadn't just knocked over a tailender: I had nicked off the best batsman in the world, who had scored 215 against us in the second Test, in my first over back. After being hit for four the previous ball, the sense of relief was overwhelming.

That early wicket and release of emotion was enough to settle me down, and I felt just like I had against Somerset two weeks previously: I saw every ball as an opportunity to get a wicket, rather than worrying about my economy rate and the prospect of getting hit for four. I struck again in my third over with a yorker that was as much of a surprise to me as it was to Michael Clarke, whose feet were stuck on the crease. I landed the ball much fuller than I had intended, but it fizzed beneath the toe of his bat and thudded into his stumps. I couldn't have dreamed of a better start: I had two wickets in my first 14 balls back in Test cricket, Australia's best batter and then their captain. I was full of adrenaline, and my pace was up: I hit Chris Rogers, my old Middlesex teammate, on the elbow, and he pulled a face at me that confirmed it felt quick to him, too. I'd bowled at him in the nets and as a younger player, but this was the first time we'd faced one another in a competitive game for years. He told me later on that he'd found that first spell I bowled to him genuinely scary.

The first day was interrupted by rain, and every time we left the field I was itching to get back out there again as soon as possible. I felt on top of the world after those two wickets: we were miles on top of the game, taking three early wickets after Australia chose to bat first, and I was desperate to keep bowling. As it happened, I only ended up bowling 10 overs in the innings: Jimmy ran through their lower order to take 6 for 47, and we bowled Australia out for 136. It was an incredible feeling to walk off with Jimmy leading us back to the dressing room and soaking in the atmosphere: I always loved playing international cricket at Edgbaston, and the intensity of the Ashes made it even more special.

I was expecting some chatter from the Aussies when I walked out to bat on the second day: David Warner duly obliged, asking his teammates when they'd send me home this time (or words to that effect). We knew each other back from his time at Middlesex in 2010 and had played against each other a lot since, so I knew he wasn't deadly serious, but it was just a reminder that the 2013/14 tour had stuck in other people's memories, not just my own. I was lucky, in a sense, that Australia had become a very different team from the one I had first encountered: Ricky Ponting and Brad Haddin would have been up and at me straight away, but their close fielders were not as abrasive and aggressive as I expected when I walked out. The fact that we were a long way ahead in the game probably helped, as half-centuries from Joe Root, Ian Bell and Moeen Ali gave us a 145-run first-innings lead.

The rest of that day was like a dream: a decade on, people still come up to me and tell me that they were at Edgbaston to see it. It started inauspiciously: my first over cost 14 runs, with Warner coming out fired up. He must have sensed the chance to get under my skin, because he was sledging me relentlessly: after every ball, he'd tell me what speed he thought I was bowling in kilometres per hour. '122.' '121.' 'Well done mate, that one was up at 126.' It was another clever bit of man management from Cooky that sorted me out. He decided that I should change ends, and that I'd be more effective from the Pavilion End than from the City End; two balls into my spell, I got Smith out for the second time in the match. It might have been the worst ball that I bowled that day, short and wide outside his off stump, but he had a huge swipe at it, trying to pull me in to the on side, and top-edged it straight up in the air. Much like the first innings, where the ball hung forever in the air to Cooky, this one felt like it went to the moon and I was watching it come back down towards Jos. It felt like another massive moment in the Test match, and I was ecstatic to be at the centre of it. The best batsman in the world out twice in a game? I'll take that.

The crowd were in good voice when we came back out after tea: the Eric Hollies Stand at Edgbaston is always lively, filled with fancy dress, and tends to get more and more boisterous as the day wears on. It had reached the time in the day that Spiderman starts climbing the stands, or a group of butchers chase a pig around the aisles. I loved playing for England at Lord's – there was the sentimental value of the fact it was my home ground, in addition to the obvious history and tradition – but Edgbaston was my favourite international venue because of that raucous atmosphere. I'm not sure I'd ever felt more attuned to a crowd than in my first over of that evening session: the whole stand roared in celebration when I had Clarke caught at second slip, and then erupted when Adam Voges edged his first ball to third slip. The place went crazy: I was running away celebrating, getting mobbed by my teammates, and the noise was unbelievable. If I could relive any single moment of my international career, it would be standing at the top of my mark and preparing to bowl my hat-trick ball to Mitchell Marsh. It felt like the whole of Birmingham, let alone Edgbaston, was egging me on. I bowled another big outswinger which he left alone, but I felt certain that I'd get him out sooner rather than later: I was having so much fun and feeding off the crowd's energy as I raced into the crease. Warner's sledging had long since stopped.

I had the thing that I craved more than any other across my career: control. I was bowling fast – consistently in the high 80s – and the ball went wherever I wanted it to. I could run up thinking, 'This is going to be a bit shorter than the last one, swinging away with steep bounce,' and everything that I tried, worked. I was never a metronome like Jimmy, who could run up and land the ball on a sixpence. I was a confidence, rhythm and feel bowler, and in that spell, my confidence was higher than it had ever been before. Marsh could hardly lay a bat on me: I beat him on the outside edge, had a very good lbw shout turned down and then cleaned him up with one that nipped back through the gate. I was all over Peter Nevill, the wicketkeeper who had replaced Haddin: he played and missed three times in a row as the crowd roared me to the crease. Bowling felt effortless: it was like the crowd's energy was carrying me, to the extent that I wasn't using any of my own. I could have bowled the entire day, no problem.

I came back for another burst before the close of play and struck with my first ball: it was just meant to be for me that day. Johnson went to pull but his steepling top edge looped up to Ben Stokes at point, giving me my fifth wicket of the innings. It was my first Test match five-wicket haul against Australia since my first appearance in the Ashes, back at the Gabba in 2010, but it was the first time that I had properly run through their line-up. I was fully in love with cricket again. I had spent so much of my England career looking over my shoulder, worrying about my economy rate or putting myself under pressure that I had lost sight of the fact that the reason I did this for a living was because I loved the sport for its own sake, and the feeling of bowling fast. It is hard to do when you are caught up in the bubble of international sport, with so much stuff happening around you and ever more going on inside your own head, but I was incredibly proud to be back in an England Test shirt. All of the small things that I had taken for granted about playing Test cricket – standing for the national anthems, and hearing 'Jerusalem' played at the start of each day – I made sure to embrace.

When I led the team off the field that evening, I had figures of 5 for 45 and felt on top of the world; Australia led by 23 with three wickets left in their second innings, and it was only a question of when, not if, we would win. I couldn't sleep: I was too excited to get back out there. I was lying wide awake in bed and felt like there was electricity running through my body. All I wanted to do was to walk back down to Edgbaston from our hotel in the centre of Birmingham, strap my boots on and start bowling again. I was getting too far ahead of myself, imagining myself taking the final three wickets for an Ashes eight-for, but I could hardly help it: everything that I had dreamed about for the previous two years had happened in the last two days.

The adrenaline didn't let up all night, and I was knackered when I arrived at the ground on the third morning. We were a long way ahead in the game, but the Aussies made us work hard: Jimmy was off the field with a side strain and I started the day with a seven-over spell. Nevill and Mitchell Starc played their shots and put a small dent in my figures, but I took my sixth wicket when Jos took a brilliant diving catch down the leg side to get Nevill and finished with 6 for 79, my new career-best in Tests. I led the team off the field for the second day in a row, holding the ball aloft as the crowd stood and applauded, then watched us knock off the target of 121 in just over 30 overs to win the match and take a 2–1 lead in the series. I sat in the dressing room with the match ball, and with my man-of-the-match medal on, and reflected on what I'd just achieved – and how proud I felt to have got back to the top. We spent the whole afternoon in there, sharing a few beers and enjoying the highlights on TV, then went into Birmingham to continue the celebrations. Those were three of the best days of my cricketing life.

The only thing I struggled with that week was the press. I did the media rounds on the second evening, and my face was on the back page of every newspaper the following morning after my five-for. It felt like every single journalist had written the same thing: Steven Finn has gone from unselectable to unplayable. It pissed me off. I wanted to celebrate my achievement for what it was, rather than it being used as an opportunity to remind everyone about the mess I had been in eighteen months previously. I'm not stupid: I understood why that was the story after they had all questioned whether I'd ever play again. And there were a lot of nice things written that week too, about the hard work that I'd put in behind the scenes and the resilience I'd shown to make it back to the top. But the way it was framed rubbed me up the wrong way: I wanted people to write about how well I'd bowled, swinging the ball away from right-handers and running through Australia's middle order, rather than something that I felt I had put behind me.

The first morning of the fourth Test at Trent Bridge was completely surreal. There had been a lot of talk in the build-up about how we would cope without Jimmy, whose side strain ruled him out of the last two Tests, and Mark Wood came back into the side to replace him. Broady had a rare opportunity to bowl the first over of the match, and made a point in the build-up of telling everyone that he was going to set the tone for us. Jimmy was an assassin, with control like no other bowler I've ever seen. His intrinsic skills of fast bowling were so far advanced compared to anyone else I'd played with. But Broady was a warrior. He was skilful and intelligent in his own right, but I've never seen someone have the same impact in single spells as he had. You could tell when it was about to happen: he had this look in his eyes where you could see he was concentrating incredibly hard, and he absolutely steamed into the crease that morning. It was the best toss that Cook ever won: perfect bowling conditions, with lush green grass on the pitch and perfect tennis-ball bounce. Broady took full advantage. Right from the first ball that he bowled, you could tell that he was on one: he was running in so hard that his knees were up around his ears, and he was totally unplayable that day. It felt like no one would score a run against him, he was so fired up.

When I was brought on to bowl the eighth over, Australia were 27 for 6 and Broad already had five wickets, all of them caught in the slips – including Stokes's spectacular one-handed grab to get Voges. It was electrifying to be out there and part of it, and another incredible Ashes atmosphere at Trent Bridge to follow Edgbaston the week before. I felt great with the ball in my hand again, and bowled what was probably the best ball of my Test career among the carnage at the other end. I drew Nevill half-forward with an outswinger, which then nipped back in late off the seam, through the gap between bat and pad, and smashed into the top of his off stump. Unsurprisingly, it was totally overshadowed: Broad wrapped up the tail to finish with ridiculous figures of 8 for 15, and we bowled Australia out for 60. It was a similar opening day to the Melbourne Test in 2010/11, except this time I felt fully part of it. We sat in the dressing room that evening with a lead of more than 200 and six first-innings wickets in hand and thought, 'We've got this one in the bag.'

I made sure to soak up the rest of that Test match: we declared just before lunch on the second day with a lead of more than 300, and I'm not sure I had ever felt so confident that I would win a game of cricket. We were absolutely all over them, and knew that our attack was too good for them in those conditions, so could stand on the outfield, look around at the packed crowd and enjoy the occasion. I had already been part of two Ashes wins, but had been running the drinks in 2010/11 and only turned up for the celebrations in 2013 after being dropped. I had longed for the feeling of being out there in the middle with my teammates as we put the finishing touches to a series victory, and knew that it was just a matter of time until it arrived. Stokes bowled amazingly on that second day, hooping the ball away from their left-handers, and we walked off that night three wickets away.

It felt just as good as I had always imagined when Woody wrapped things up on the third morning. That whole day was amazing: we won the Test inside the first hour, but most of the crowd stayed deep into the afternoon to be a part of the celebrations, and I couldn't wipe the smile off my face as I wandered around the stands, signing autographs and posing for pictures. There was even a fly-over from the Red Arrows. I spotted my parents in the crowd during our lap of the ground, and the sight of my dad's eyes watering was almost enough to set me off on the spot. I'd never seen him so emotional and pushed through the crowd to give both of them hugs. We made a big effort that summer to reconnect with the ex-players who were working in the media – guys like Bob Willis and Ian Botham – to get them off our backs and help them feel like they were tied to the present, and also made sure that players' families were involved. They all came up to the dressing room at Trent Bridge to celebrate with us: it was an acknowledgement of the sacrifices that they had made for all of us along the way, and I was incredibly proud to share that special moment with them.

The Oval Test was a strange one: an anticlimax after the euphoria of back-to-back wins – especially since they had been so emphatic, both finishing inside three days. But I still saw it as another opportunity to play for my country after missing so many Tests – and to further prove myself ahead of the upcoming series against Pakistan and South Africa. Broady came up to me on the first day, as Australia were piling on the runs, and said, 'Jeez, this is flat, isn't it?' Honestly, I didn't mind at all: I just wanted to bowl. I grafted seriously hard in that innings, getting into my 30th over, and was chuffed to finish with 3 for 90. I also finally ticked off a milestone that had been a long time coming: after two years stuck on 90 Test wickets, I had reached 99 in no time but twice had my 100th struck off for a front-foot no-ball, once at Trent Bridge and then again at The Oval. I was never a big one for personal milestones, but I was aware of my numbers and breathed a big sigh of relief when Mitchell Marsh edged me to second slip.

Our batters struggled badly and we lost by an innings, but I wasn't going to let that derail the celebrations. Just like the winning moment at Trent Bridge had, standing on the podium and spraying champagne around felt very different to 2010/11 and 2013: I knew that I had contributed a lot to the series win. The two sets of players shared a beer in the dressing rooms as usual: Root and Warner made a point of making up after that night in Birmingham two years previously, and I made sure to seek Johnson out to make him aware of just how much our conversation eighteen months earlier had meant to me. We swapped shirts and left each other messages. His read: 'To Steve, Congrats on your 100th. Many more to come. Be your best, mate!!' We had a great night out in London: I still have a picture saved on my phone of the Ashes urn in a nightclub next to two bottles of Belvedere vodka.

We knew that we weren't the finished article by any means as an England team, but we had still been good enough to beat Australia across a topsy-turvy series. There was a core of young players in that team – Root, Stokes, Buttler and Jonny Bairstow – who had been around international cricket for a little while but were starting to become an integral part of the set-up; I was only a year or two older than most of them, but had been around for long enough that I felt like I had been welcomed back as a more senior player. The thing that I really cherished in that series was how much the coaching set-up – Bayliss, Farbrace and Gibson in particular – made me feel really valued and wanted, more so than I ever had been previously. There had been times in an England environment where all I'd wanted was for someone to come up to me and say, 'We love you. We think you're great.' I'd subliminally built up all these inhibitions over the previous five years, constantly worrying about getting hit for four. If I bowled a bad over in that series, Trevor would just tell me, 'You'll wake up tomorrow, you'll still be breathing, and life moves on.' It sounds so simple, but it was a management style that I responded so well to, and it gave me such a liberated approach to Test cricket.

Sport is funny. You move on so quickly to the next thing that you never quite have enough time to dwell on your success or realise its significance until much later. It is hard to be fully present in any given moment when the schedule is so relentless, with no time to breathe. A week after that final Test match, we were down in Cardiff playing a T20 international, and the world moved on. Smith hit me for a massive six over square leg in that game, and screamed, 'That's huge, son!' at me as he struck it. How the tables had turned since Edgbaston. That Ashes series felt special straight away, but it was only with time and distance that I realised what a highlight it would be in my career. In the moment, I just saw it as a springboard: I was back, and my international career was only going one way. I'd had my down, which every player has. I was twenty-six years old, still young in sporting terms, and my body was holding up well. I was strong, fit and confident. Why would this not be the first step towards bigger and better things?

With the benefit of hindsight, this would prove to be a peak for me – my own personal Everest, which took all my resilience and determination to scale. But I did it. I made it all the way back to the top, to where I dreamed of being and where I was so driven to prove that I belonged. Regardless of what happened next, I wouldn't trade that for the world.

# 11

# Injury Strikes

I was bowling with Jimmy Anderson in the nets in Abu Dhabi, two days out from our Test series against Pakistan in late 2015, when I felt a searing pain in my foot like nothing I had ever experienced before. 'Oh shit,' I thought to myself. I knew straight away that this was bad.

I'd been feeling brilliant since we touched down in the United Arab Emirates. I had bowled unbelievably well in a warm-up game against Pakistan A in Sharjah soon after we landed: my figures were 4 for 16 from 15 overs and I was in true, absolute control. It wasn't so long ago that I had felt miles away from this, but now my flow and rhythm were back. Bowling was incredibly fun again. I have never thought that I deserved anything, but after the lows that I had experienced, I felt like I had finally earned the opportunity to have a run in the team.

Heading into that tour, I wasn't certain if I'd be selected. There was a chance that we would change the balance of our side at the cost of a seamer, and with Jimmy, Stuart Broad and Mark Wood all back fit, there was a possibility that I might be squeezed out for the first Test. But I was super confident that I was not only worth my place, but in a spot where I could really cement it by helping England win Test matches.

I made sure to run in hard during training and leave as good an impression on Trevor Bayliss, our coach, as possible.

I'd had some discomfort in my foot towards the end of the home summer, but didn't think too much of it because I could play through it. If the issue was fairly gruesome, it was nothing that I wasn't used to as a fast bowler. In essence, the toenail of the big toe on my left foot was lifting and then digging into the nail bed: it was painful and exacerbated by the harder pitches in the UAE, but something that I thought I could manage. The trouble was that subconsciously, I was modifying the way that my foot landed in order to try to stop it hurting so much. I was lifting my big toe as my front foot was landing in my delivery stride, and putting extra pressure on the ball of my foot. I knew something wasn't quite right, but there was no way in hell that I was going to let an issue with my toenail rule me out of a Test match. I told myself I was going to get through it, and that if I loaded up on as many painkillers as our medical team would let me, I'd be absolutely fine. It even reached the point where we were using numbing creams and considering injecting it with anaesthetic.

But there I was, bowling in training with Jimmy, when I felt that sharp pain through my left foot. It was agony. I tried to bowl another ball, but it hurt so badly that I couldn't even run up to the crease. I felt panicked: I knew this wasn't good, but I was desperate to play in the first Test. I couldn't miss another opportunity, especially when I was in such a good rhythm and bowling so well. Jimmy looked sympathetic but said, 'Mate, you've got to stop here. Don't be an idiot and make it worse than it already is.' I went over to see our team doctor, a guy called Rob Young, and showed him just how much of a mess my big toe was, with blood everywhere underneath the nail. That wasn't the issue in itself, but the source of it: the real problem was the way that I had modified the way I was landed on my left foot as a result.

Rob took me off for a scan that afternoon, and the results were not good. I'd effectively cracked the ball of my foot, creating a stress fracture through the middle of it. Not only could I not bowl, I couldn't bear any weight on it. He delivered the news to me at the ground, and the photographer Gareth Copley captured the exact moment that I was told my tour was over. I looked utterly forlorn and downbeat, as you'd expect. The best-case scenario, Rob told me, was that I'd be fit for Christmas time, when we were due to be in South Africa. I was out of the Pakistan Tests, and out of the one-day and T20 series that followed. I had climbed that mountain to get back into the Test team in the summer and was finally ready to run with my opportunity, to grow in confidence and become settled in the side, but the rug had cruelly been ripped out from under my feet again.

I sat down with Trevor for a coffee in the hotel lobby before my flight home and told him how gutted I was to be leaving the tour early. I felt like I was ahead of Woody in the pecking order at the time, and he confirmed to me that I would have been picked not only for the first Test, but probably the whole series because of how well I'd been bowling. It was a bittersweet moment: confirmation that he saw me playing a prominent role in his team, but hard to take knowing that I would have had an opportunity which was snatched away through no fault of my own. My mentality was that everyone had a tricky period in their career, even if mine had been a bit more extreme than most, and that I had overcome it. I was twenty-six, and ready to nail my spot down once and for all. After the mental anguish of hitting the lows that I had, after two years out of the team, after all the work that I'd done to get myself into contention, I had now been robbed of the chance that I felt I had truly earned.

I sat at home and watched that series on TV with my foot in a big protective boot. Once the initial disappointment of coming home had worn off, I tried to avoid being too down in the dumps about it. There was nothing I could do to change what had happened, but I could make sure that I stuck diligently to my rehabilitation plan to ensure I would be fit for the first Test in South Africa, in Durban on Boxing Day. I had to have my big toenail completely removed, too: I couldn't feel a thing, with my foot obscured by a screen and the pain numbed by local anesthetic, but didn't enjoy seeing the doctor walking off with my nail between his pliers. The doctors even considered removing the nailbed altogether, so that I would never have a big toenail again, but thankfully decided against it. When I returned to playing, I had something made for me that was effectively a hard, plastic toenail: I would strap it to my left big toe as protection, in case I got hit on the boot by a yorker while I was batting.

I did a lot of my rehab at the Watford FC training ground in London Colney. They'd just been promoted back into the Premier League and I had a good relationship with the club at the time: they knew that I was a lifelong fan, and would sort me out with tickets whenever I needed them. Mum first took me to watch them play just after my seventh birthday, a 6–3 win over Grimsby Town, and I was hooked: I was even the mascot a few years later, for a defeat at Southampton. As my cricketing career took off, I got to meet a few of the players, like Tom Cleverley, Troy Deeney and Ben Watson. I was chatting to Scott Duxbury, the chief executive, at Vicarage Road after coming back from the UAE and no sooner had I mentioned my injury, he was inviting me into the training ground. Watford had the piece of equipment that I had been looking for without success: an AlterG machine, effectively an anti-gravity treadmill that takes most of your body weight off you and allows you to run even if you have a foot injury.

The ECB had a sponsorship deal with Toyota at the time, and I'd not got around to fixing up the bumps and scrapes on my Rav4 before heading away for the winter. It meant pulling into the training ground and parking between a Lamborghini and an Aston Martin, while my wing mirror was held together by black duct tape. All of Watford's expensive summer signings must have wondered who this six feet eight inch new face was, as I lay down on the bed next to Deeney on my first morning there and got a foot massage from the head physio. It was a surreal few weeks heading in and rubbing shoulders every day with the players that I was used to watching from the stands, but I was incredibly grateful to the club: the England physios were all overseas with the senior squad, so Watford's generosity really came in handy.

The first major step in my comeback was to join the England Lions tour to the UAE, where I played a couple of T20s against Pakistan A to prove my fitness. It meant I was reunited with Andy Flower, who had taken charge of the Lions after leaving his England job, and I was struck by how much he had changed. It felt like he had calmed down a lot – he certainly evolved as a coach as his career went on – and it was nice to spend a bit of time working with him again. I remembered the compassion that he had shown me on the Australia tour in 2013/14, and particularly the conversation we'd had at Alice Springs airport when he took me out of contention for selection to try and help me get things right. At the gym in Dubai, he looked me up and down and told me, 'You look fit and strong!' with a smile on his face. I must be doing something right if Andy Flower is complimenting me, I thought.

That's not to say he was no longer intense. Flower had a habit of singling people out in team meetings to ask them their views, which was his way of forcing people to think about the game: he wanted his players to engage fully with the team and think on their feet, rather than just playing on autopilot. I watched him choose young players, who were caught on the hop, and realised that I was at a very different stage in my career to them. It reminded me of being sat there minding my own business as a 21-year-old and being asked, 'Finn! What did you think of KP's shot in the first innings?' I was now treated slightly differently, as a fully fledged England player dropping down into the Lions squad to prove my fitness, and sat there knowing that I could rest easy.

That encounter with Flower made me think about the different coaching styles that I had experienced, and which ones I responded to best. The thing that Trevor had, which I loved, was an ability to make international cricket not seem like a big deal. When I was coming back into the Test team, I found that incredibly helpful. He was so encouraging. He picked players like Alex Hales and James Vince because he wanted them to be aggressive at the top of the order, and it was similar for bowlers: he would tell me that he only cared about wickets, and he wanted me in his team because I was a wicket-taking bowler. I really responded to that style. Paul Farbrace, his assistant coach, was a good influence for me too: where Trevor was a quiet observer, Farby was uber-positive, and would go around pumping people's tyres up. At that stage in my career, that was something I responded to really well, and their mix of coaching styles helped me to find my best self during that period.

Flower was very different: an intense, strong character who preached discipline and control, and wanted you to fit into a certain role rather than moulding his team to individuals' traits. When I look back, I would love to have played under Trevor Bayliss more, just as I would love to have played under Brendon McCullum and Ben Stokes's leadership. I look at the way England have played under those two, with their explicit focus on taking wickets, and imagine the completely different international career I might have had if they had been in charge when I was twenty or twenty-one years old. But equally, the team that I came into in 2010 probably needed a strong character as head coach. There were some big personalities in that changing room, and it might not have functioned in the way that it did – with a clear tactical approach, and a common goal – if we'd had a more relaxed character in charge. Would we have reached number 1 in the world with a different coach? Would we have won the 2010/11 Ashes in Australia, then retained them on home soil in 2013? I doubt we would have without a coach like Flower, and those were such significant milestones in my career that I wouldn't want to change them – and I am sure that would be echoed by almost everyone who played in that team.

I hit the ground running on that stopover in Dubai. I was hitting the track hard, swinging the ball, and found bowling really fun again. I felt as though I picked up where I had left off. I was jumping through the hoops that I needed to in order to get on that tour to South Africa and, thankfully, the stars aligned. I hadn't been named in the initial squad for that Test series, which gave me added motivation: I felt like I knew my body better than anyone else, and I always enjoyed having the chance to prove people wrong. I was added to the squad when I was passed fit, and made it down there for the last warm-up match ahead of the first Test. I bowled well down in Pietermaritzburg, taking six wickets, and felt confident of forcing my way into the team for Boxing Day even before Jimmy Anderson went down injured. I was in great rhythm immediately and felt like a massive part of the squad. I approached the whole series with a different mindset: I wasn't playing to impress anyone, or to make sure that I was in the team for the next Test match; I was playing like I had earned the right to be there, with my sole focus on how I could help England win.

I got the nod that I had been expecting, and was immediately excited to play in a Boxing Day Test. After all, it was the first time I'd been picked for one: following the disappointment of missing out in 2010, I had been nowhere near selection in the only one since, three years later on the 2013/14 tour. Our winter schedules mean that most England cricketers will only get a handful of chances to play in a Boxing Day Test, and this was mine. Even if the MCG – one of the world's most iconic cricket stadiums – is the gold standard, then I knew that it would be an amazing occasion in South Africa, too.

The build-up was weird: my family hadn't travelled – my parents and sister never saw me play an overseas Test match – and I didn't have a girlfriend at the time, so I was sitting on a table with guys who were also single, or whose family weren't able to make it, at the team hotel, pulling crackers with James Taylor and Chris Jordan. It was all a bit surreal, but I was just counting down to the following morning in my head. Our last Test series against South Africa in 2012 was the only one that I'd played a match in and lost, and while they had slipped down the world rankings since, they still had a seriously strong side and plenty of world-class players: Hashim

Amla, AB de Villiers, Dale Steyn and Morne Morkel. It felt like a shot at redemption, both for the team and for me personally.

De Villiers was one of the best batsmen in the world at that time, and I felt like I grew a couple of inches in my first spell of the match when I had him hopping around. The pitch in Durban really suited me: there was good bounce in the first innings, and I got the ball nipping about. In my second over, I got one to leap off a good length and smash the splice of de Villiers' bat. He took his bottom hand off the handle and the ball flew into the gully where Ben Stokes dived forward, but didn't claim the catch. He wasn't sure whether or not it had carried and the TV replays were inconclusive – though I'm sure if he had claimed it, it would have been given out. I always loved the feeling of hitting players on the splice of the bat, and seeing them flinch as the ball rattled into it and made the handle vibrate. Seeing de Villiers react like that was the moment that I thought, 'Right, I'm into my work here.' I felt awesome, and even though I only took a couple of wickets in South Africa's first innings, I knew that I had bowled well and played a part in us taking a decent first-innings lead. This series was the only time in my career that I noticed a batsman change his technique just for me. From the second Test onwards, when de Villiers faced me, he would go really deep in his crease and across his stumps, inviting me to try to pitch the ball fuller. He realised that my strength was hitting the pitch but that I wouldn't be able to do that if he continually played off the back foot, forcing me to try to go fuller where I floated it up a bit more and was less effective.

We set South Africa 416 to win in the fourth innings, and after a couple of expensive overs to start, I broke their resistance in my second spell. I was flowing to the crease effortlessly, getting a bit of help from the pitch, and was creating chances all the time: I had Amla caught behind, beat de Villiers with my first ball to him, and then had Dean Elgar edging to second slip. When I was brought back for one final spell on the fourth evening, the light was fading and the ball was reverse swinging. Faf du Plessis had dug in resiliently, but conditions were perfectly suited for me: I got one to bounce that little bit more than anyone else had managed to, took the shoulder of his bat, and the ball flew to Alastair Cook at slip. Paul Farbrace would always tell me that was his favourite wicket he saw me take for England, because of the match situation and the fact that I'd managed to find that extra bounce in the final over of the day. We wrapped up the win the following morning, and I finished with match figures of 6 for 91; for all my frustrations at missing out on the Pakistan series, I had slotted seamlessly back into the team and was bowling with just as much confidence as before. On the final morning I was begging Cooky to let me keep bowling to try and take my fifth wicket of the innings. He declined. I'd never find myself better set to take a five-for again in Tests.

The second Test was at Newlands, in Cape Town, a ground that I first visited on the England Under-16s tour that really ignited my desire to play international cricket. It was an incredibly beautiful setting, but an incredibly flat pitch that week. We batted first and I spent the first day and a half watching from the dressing room as Stokes and Jonny Bairstow put on 399 as a partnership, smashing the ball everywhere. Right from the first warm-up game of the tour, this looked like a different Ben Stokes. Given the responsibility of batting at number six by Bayliss, he responded by playing one of the most dominating, destructive innings I have ever seen. It was completely savage: we watched from the balcony in awe at the shots up and over wide long-off for six. But the wicket was a pancake. South

Africa tried to grind us into the dirt and did a seriously good job of it: I got through 39 overs, the most I'd ever bowled in a single innings – for England or Middlesex – and was beyond exhausted by the time they finally declared with the scores more or less level. I had de Villiers caught at midwicket, and Chris Morris smashed a tired length ball to cover. I'm not sure I had ever had to work as hard for two wickets. They kept us in the field for 211 overs – yes, 211 – but whenever I felt particularly tired, I would look up at Table Mountain in the backdrop and remind myself how lucky I was to be playing at such an incredible venue. If there was any ground in the world where I had to spend that long in the field, then Newlands was top of the list.

We clinched the series with a win at the Wanderers in Johannesburg. There was pace and carry in the pitch again: I would bowl balls on what felt like a good-to-full length, and then the steepling bounce would mean they ended up hitting the splice or the shoulder of the bat. The pitches in South Africa were amazing to bowl on: they suited my pace and height perfectly.

By my mid-twenties, I'd played enough international cricket that there were some players I had faced a lot. Some guys, like David Warner and Kane Williamson, always seemed to score runs off me, but there were others whom I had a happy knack of getting out. Hashim Amla was one of them: I got him in both innings of the Lord's Test in 2012, and I turned him inside out at the Wanderers, too. Nasser Hussain must have watched and commentated on almost all of the Tests I played in, and said on Sky Sports that he had never seen me bowl as well as I did in that game, even though my figures (2 for 50) probably didn't show it. I got Amla with a ball that angled in on a fullish length, bounced sharply and angled away off the seam, and took the outside edge as I squared him up. The carry on the pitch meant it hung in the air forever before it was caught behind. We led by 10 runs after both teams had batted once, just before lunch on the third day, then won the Test match later that day thanks to one of Broad's trademark spells. I could see in his eyes again that he was totally locked in, with his knees pumping high, and he ran through their batting line-up, taking 6 for 17. We knocked the runs off in the evening session, and toasted a series win with a game to spare.

But I couldn't celebrate with the same enthusiasm as everyone else. I felt in such great rhythm in that series and was determined to make the most of it, but during South Africa's second innings, I had gone off injured. I bowled a ball and felt like I had been winded: I had a sharp pain in my side and felt short of breath. I finished the over but I couldn't get through my action properly. I had my side strapped up, completely covered in blue tape all over my ribs to try and support the muscles underneath, but couldn't bowl again and went for a scan at the end of the Test match. I had a grade two tear in my side, and knew I would be stuffed for quite a while.

It was a cruel blow, which made me feel like I'd had my wings clipped again. What had I done to deserve this? It was another major frustration. Trevor Bayliss told me that I'd been our best bowler of the series to that point. Jimmy had an uncharacteristically quiet series and if Broad had been devastating in that spell, I had provided the most consistent threat. I was the standout, but felt completely dejected as I sat in the dressing room, fighting back the annoyance of knowing that I'd be out of action for a considerable amount of time. I still felt confident that I would be back involved in the summer, but it was so frustrating. I'd not missed many Test matches through injury in my career – those three Tests on the India tour in 2012 were the exception to the rule – but suddenly, I was going to miss the last one in South Africa which would make it four out of seven that winter that I was injured for. I took 11 wickets in three Tests: how many could it have been if I'd played all seven, given the confidence that I had and the rhythm I was in? I hated the fact that my body was letting me down.

Trevor didn't send me straight home, and I was glad he didn't. I was gutted to have missed the celebrations when we won the 2012 series in India, when I went back early to spend a few extra days at home, and decided that I'd stick around. I'd played a massive part in helping us win the series, after all, and it was a significant milestone in my career to beat South Africa, especially in their own backyard. At the time, I was an ambassador for Investec, the South African bank who sponsored Test series in England, and they invited me down to a big horse race down in Cape Town: Trevor was brilliant, and was happy for me to head down there for a couple of days while the rest of the squad travelled to Centurion for the last Test. He knew that I was gutted to be missing out, and needed to clear my head as much as possible. That whole tour was an amazing experience: I made a point of trying to enjoy the off-field side of it as much as I could. We lost the last Test convincingly, but I was glad I stayed back to celebrate the series win with the guys – even if I felt a bit like John Terry lifting the trophy in my full England whites on the last day.

My injury meant that I was out of the one-day and T20 legs of the tour, and I was starting to feel a bit out of the loop when it came to the white-ball teams. I'd led the attack in the first home summer under Eoin Morgan's captaincy, but missing the Pakistan and South Africa series meant that I was losing out on the opportunity to keep developing my skills in those formats at a time when the team was moving forward quickly. As a result, I was chuffed to be named in the squad for the World T20 in India: it gave me something to target in my rehab from my side strain, and the prospect of playing with a dynamic, young team at a global tournament in India was a really exciting one. I could only really cycle in the first few weeks of rehab, but gradually started working towards bowling off my full run-up, and was down at the Lord's indoor school working my way back to fitness.

I was doing the most innocuous bowling drill, running up from four yards back, when I felt my calf go. I tried to bowl a couple more balls in the hope that it would sort itself out, but I couldn't. I told Richard Johnson, who was overseeing my training session, and rang the England physios to tell them what had happened. I went for a scan, which revealed a strain. It was another incredibly frustrating setback, but I was confident that I could come back from it after returning from my foot injury in good time ahead of the South Africa tour. I wasn't overly stressed by it, because I knew that the time frame would allow me to be fit and ready for the start of the World T20. All of the discussions I had with the medical team were about coming back in time for it: there was a risk I might be slightly undercooked, but I felt like I had proved with my performances leading up to the Boxing Day Test that I could hit the ground running.

I was totally bemused, then, when Angus Fraser pulled me aside in the indoor centre at Lord's while I was rehabbing. My relationship with Gus had naturally changed since he became an England selector, doubling up with his job as Middlesex's director of cricket, but we still got on very well. He said that he needed a word, and explained that England didn't want anyone going into the World T20 undercooked. They wanted everyone available from the very first warm-up game to play at 100 per cent capacity, and the medical team had told the selectors that I wouldn't be able to make that time frame. As a result, I was going to be replaced in the squad. I couldn't believe what I was hearing. 'Gus, I promise you I'll be fit enough to bowl in that World T20,' I told him. He wasn't interested. The decision has already been made, he told me. I had been ruled out, completely unnecessarily as far as I was concerned, and I was missing yet another international series because my body had let me down.

It felt unfair: I had done so many hours of strength and conditioning work in the gym since I first played for England with the explicit purpose of getting my body robust to meet the demands of international cricket. I started to question everything. Did I bowl too much two years ago, when I was trying to get my action back after the Australia tour? Was my body giving up on me at twenty-six, because of all the strain that I had put on it? They were clearly wear and tear injuries that might not have happened if I had managed my workloads differently. It was also hard to hear it from Gus, because of the relationship that I'd had with him over the years: this wasn't a conversation that we'd ever had before. It was a strange dynamic, and made me question whom I could trust: could I really be open and vulnerable with Gus if there was a chance it would be used against me in selection?

The most frustrating thing about it? I was right. I was fit again in time for the World T20. I went on Middlesex's pre-season tour to South Africa and bowled 15 overs in a warm-up match on the same day as England's opening game of the tournament against West Indies. I sat there watching it on a TV in the clubhouse at Stellenbosch, near Cape Town, and thought, 'Fucking hell, man. I should be out there.' Instead,

Liam Plunkett – who replaced me in the squad – bowled really well during that tournament and rightly became a key player in the white-ball set-up over the next few years. It was hard to comprehend when I was so headstrong and clear in my belief that I should have been there, and I found it difficult to watch that World T20. The guys played brilliantly and would have won the whole thing but for Carlos Brathwaite's incredible six-hitting in the last over of the final, but I couldn't shake the feeling that I should have been out there leading the bowling attack.

Soon after the final, I got asked to do a promotional event at my local Waitrose on Finchley Road: they were on the front of England's shirts, and this was a standard sponsor commitment where I had a few photos taken of me stacking the shelves, then spoke to a few journalists on the understanding that their write-ups would include a line about the event. Since Trevor had come in, he had encouraged us to be more open with the media: he realised, rightly, that if you remind journalists that you are a real person, not just a robot delivering a stock answer, then they would be more likely to treat you like one with what they said or wrote. I'd been sitting on my frustrations for a while and decided that I would speak my mind.

I told Paul Newman, from the *Daily Mail*, that I'd been fit to bowl for Middlesex at the start of the World T20 and that, from my perspective, it was a mistake to rule me out. 'It was frustrating,' I told him. 'The selectors had to listen to the medical people, but I don't know who got it wrong. It hasn't been explained to me.' Gus was fuming. He made me write an email to the selectors and the medical staff apologising for questioning their authority. *'Since being withdrawn from the T20 World Cup squad I have, rightly or wrongly, had a bee in my bonnet,'* I wrote. *'I was frustrated at being withdrawn and foolishly I got drawn into saying what I did. I realise the content has probably pissed off a few people who have supported me along the way. I did not mean to do that and, once again, I can only say sorry for that.'*

Of course, I knew where they were coming from: if I were a selector, would I have picked someone for a World Cup if I wasn't certain they'd be 100 per cent fit for the first game? It was just the way the whole thing played out that was so infuriating to me. I'm sure almost everyone involved understood why, and Trevor sent me a reply that I really appreciated, and which showed why I responded so well to him as a coach. *'Finny, don't apologise for being pissed off, shows you've got passion,'* he wrote. *'Use it as motivation and all will be forgotten after a few 5's in the Tests. TB.'* It was just what I needed to hear. I never felt as though my comments affected my selection in the future, because I knew how much Trevor rated me and trusted me.

But those five-wicket hauls that Trevor mentioned never came. I wish I could explain why, but I just never clicked in that 2016 summer. Even with the benefit of years of hindsight, I look back and wonder what happened to me in those few months that meant I simply couldn't recapture the rhythm, the flow and the confidence that I'd had in spades over the previous twelve months. I didn't feel like I was doing anything differently, and I still can't put my finger on exactly what went wrong. I wasn't the type of bowler who could just flick a switch and make things right, like an Anderson, who could just turn up, bowl a couple of warm-up balls and make everything slot seamlessly back into place. I knew that I had to bowl a lot in order to find my rhythm, but however much I bowled at the start of the 2016 season, it just didn't happen for me. Maybe those injuries changed something in my action that I never spotted, or maybe the continual disappointments that winter meant I was too desperate to make the most of my next opportunity. Either way, it still frustrates me now that I can't explain it.

We played Sri Lanka at the start of the summer, at a time when they were struggling to cope with the retirements of Mahela Jayawardene and Kumar Sangakkara. I took three wickets in the first Test, playing a supporting role in a comfortable win, but struggled in the second when they followed on: I took 1 for 78 from 19 overs, and didn't bowl a single maiden. Honestly, I think my biggest issue in that series was wanting it too much: I was so desperate to reassert myself after my performances in South Africa that I put a lot of pressure on myself that I really didn't need to. When you become desperate you tense up and try to force things, the very antithesis of what I was like when I was bowling well. Across that summer, I snatched at almost every opportunity I got.

I bowled much better in the third Test at Lord's, including a decent spell where the crowd had got behind me, and was put up for media duties on the third evening after taking 3 for 59. I'd always had a decent relationship with the Sky Sports commentators, and was excited to see that Michael Holding was among them that evening, microphone in hand. What was meant to be an interview ended up turning into a pep talk in front of the TV cameras; in fact, it was near enough a full-on intervention. 'You have done it in the past, Finny,' Mikey told me. 'You've taken wickets on numerous occasions, so you should rely on that past success and just go out and relax. No one can question your ability, no one can question that you deserve to be out there, so go out there, relax a bit, and get the job done.'

I walked away from it grinning, and felt a bit emotional. I was never lucky enough to watch Mikey bowl live, but I knew from all the YouTube videos I'd seen – and from the stories that people would tell about him – that he was one of the greats of the game. He was always friendly and polite to me when I saw him at games, and I felt as though he had my back on-air. It was great to have someone like that encouraging me, but I was a bit alarmed when he told me that it didn't look like I was enjoying myself. I loved playing for England so much: most of the happiest moments in my life involve being out there in my Test whites, playing with my mates and representing my country. It was a bit of a jolt and a wake-up call: I thought I was trying really hard to make the most of it, but suddenly thought, 'Am I wasting this? Do I really look miserable when I'm bowling?' It was a chastening idea that I was living my dream but not showing it.

Anderson was injured for the first Test of the second series of the summer, against Pakistan, and I wasn't quite right either. I had banged my knee while playing for Middlesex at Scarborough and it had ballooned. With hindsight, I probably shouldn't have played. I was just so desperate not to miss any more Test matches that I thought I had to. But the pain in my knee meant that I had no intensity about me: I couldn't run in with the energy that I wanted to, and bowled poorly. I had a rough week: it was the first wicketless Test of my career, and I was dropped for the next one. I was still finding it incredibly frustrating that I was bowling poorly and unable to explain why, and my luck was out, too: three of my teammates dropped catches off my bowling and when I finally thought I'd got on the board with an lbw, it was overturned on review. We were thrashed: Yasir Shah took 10 wickets for Pakistan, and their whole team celebrated by doing press-ups on the outfield in front of us. It was a total shocker, and I blamed myself.

I was dropped when Jimmy came back in for the second

Test at Old Trafford, but got the nod for the third when Stokes was unavailable. Cooky told the press that he'd been awake at 2 a.m. deciding whether to pick me or Jake Ball, who had emerged as a promising young seamer, and said that he had seen a 'glint' in my eyes when he told me I was playing. He also told them that he would encourage me not to put too much pressure on myself before that recall: 'He can worry too much about it. He cares deeply about playing for England and doesn't want to let anyone down ... You just try and tell him to relax and play.'

It was an accurate observation from someone who knew me well: Cooky was the only England player involved in every Test that I played in. It was a challenging summer in my career because I'd fought my wayback up the pecking order and could feel things slipping away from me again. From my recall in the 2015 Ashes until the end of the South Africa tour, I'd had everything that I wanted in my career: I knew that not only would I play every Test that I was available for, but that I was in such great rhythm that I would make the most of it and be an important player. But I felt that slipping away from my grasp in 2016: I was so intent on rediscovering that feeling and cared so deeply about playing for England that I was scrambling for it. My attitude, as always, was that I had to work as hard as I possibly could to make the most of the amazing opportunity I had to play for my country. I've become much more chilled out and laid back in my thirties: if I had the same outlook then and had been able to approach things in a different way, I'm sure that I would have been able to relax more and been much more likely to find that rhythm.

I bowled respectfully in the first innings, but just couldn't find a way to take a wicket. For so much of my Test career, people told me that I had a happy knack of taking wickets, even when I bowled badly; now, I couldn't take a single one even when I bowled well. I bowled 28 overs in that innings, and finally created a chance in the last of them when Rahat Ali, the Pakistan number 11, edged me straight to slip. It summed up my luck and my mood that Cooky, usually such a safe pair of hands, put it down. At the end of the day, after three wicketless innings in a row, Cooky stood up in the dressing room and singled me out for my effort. 'I know it was a really hard day, but I want to talk about somebody who didn't take any wickets today,' he said. 'Finny absolutely charged in, gave everything, and didn't have any rewards.' It was the complete opposite to the start of my career, when David Saker reminded me that I'd been lucky to take six-for at the Gabba in my first Ashes Test despite not bowling well. The contrast was stark. I think I know which one I'd prefer.

I finally got my rewards in the second innings. We conceded a lead of 103 on first innings, but the guys batted brilliantly to set Pakistan a target of 343 batting last. Their top order were making a decent fist of it but we got the ball reversing, and things started to click for me. I had Misbah-ul-Haq caught behind with one that tailed away from him late, and my celebration was one of the loudest of my career, screaming 'come on' as a weight lifted from my shoulders. I clearly loved a big celebration at Edgbaston. Cooky punched the air at first slip, too, knowing how much it meant to me – and how important the wicket was for the team. I then removed Sami Aslam, the left-handed opener: after setting him up with a series of away swingers from around the wicket, I reversed one back into him, which pinged into the top of his off stump. It was a huge relief as much as anything after such a poor series from an individual perspective, and I was buzzing to have contributed something to another Test win. My post-match media duties consisted of an interview with Chris Woakes, reflecting on how we'd been room-mates in 2008 for the Under-19s and were now both taking wickets to help England win a Test match.

But it was back down to earth with a thud at The Oval. We were still in transition as a side and Pakistan were a tough team to play against: Asad Shafiq scored a hundred, Younis Khan made a double, and they took a lead of more than 200 in the first innings to set up a series-levelling win. We set them a pitiful target of 40 to win on the fourth day, and with nothing to lose, Cooky opened the bowling with me and Woakesy – who had a brilliant summer, his breakthrough year in Test cricket – rather than Anderson and Broad. After two balls, I felt my hamstring go 'ping' and had to walk off midway through my first over. It was my fourth injury in a twelve-month period, and left me wondering if my body would ever be quite the same again.

James Whitaker, one of the England selectors, sat me down after that Test and told me that I would miss the one-day series that followed. He framed it to me by saying that I would probably have been left out anyway, and that my injury just confirmed that I needed a break. Clearly, they had spoken about the fact that I was beating myself up and trying too hard, and it ended up being the beginning of the end of my ODI career: all of a sudden, I hadn't played a limited-overs international in the last year, and Morgs's white-ball team had moved on without me.

But there was a silver lining to missing out on that series. Thankfully, my hamstring injury wasn't as serious as first feared and, three weeks later, I was back playing for Middlesex in our title run-in at the end of the County Championship season. I took seven wickets in our win over Nottinghamshire at Trent Bridge, and we drew away at Lancashire to leave our last game, against Yorkshire, as a title decider. As it was meandering towards a draw on the final day – which would have made Somerset champions – the captains left the field and negotiated in the bathroom at the back of the home dressing rooms. They eventually settled on a target: we would send down enough slow lobs from our batsmen to leave a target of 240 in 40 overs.

I get why some people don't like contrived declarations, but they are part of what makes cricket unique, and made for an amazing day's play. County cricket can be a tough grind at times, trying to find some motivation when playing in front of a few hundred fans, but there were about 7,000 at Lord's that afternoon as the sun set behind the Warner Stand and the vast majority of them cared deeply about Middlesex. Once they realised that there was going to be a result one way or the other, there was an incredible buzz in the stands on an amazing last afternoon in the setting sun. We had 40 overs to take 10 wickets, and Toby Roland-Jones was in such good rhythm that I was bowling from the Nursery End: it was never my preference, but Toby was on a roll. Yorkshire kept on swinging: Toby finished the job with a hat-trick, spread across two overs, and I rugby-tackled him to the ground to start a whole squad pile-on as he ran down to fine leg celebrating.

It was the culmination of a project that had been building for many years at Middlesex: it reminded me why I played the game, and why cricket could be so special. I celebrated with some of my closest mates – Roland-Jones, Sam Robson, Tim Murtagh and many others – and reflected on the turnaround at the club under Angus Fraser. We were stragglers towards the bottom of Division 2 when Gus took over as director of cricket in 2009, but he assembled a squad and a group of people he believed in, took us up and made us competitors. That day – our first Championship win since 1993 – was the result of all of his hard work. I had missed a lot of Middlesex games on England duty over the years, but the club felt special to me: it was my home, after all, and I knew how much time and effort guys like Gus and Richard Johnson had invested in my career. Anyone connected with the club piled into the dressing room: we had Gus and Mike Gatting doing 'shoe bombs' – Jägerbombs served in Tim Murtagh's bowling boots. We started the night in the Lord's Tavern pub that we'd frequented so regularly in the years preceding, singing with the supporters and pouring our own pints behind the bar, then moved on to some dancing in a bar in Camden in our playing whites.

It was a special way to finish what had been a difficult year personally. From the highs of the previous summer, my Ashes comeback, and a strong series in South Africa, I had spent the season chasing my tail. Even though I felt like I was stubborn and resilient enough to overcome another setback, the warning signs had started to emerge.

# 12

# The Beginning of the End

Andrew Strauss sat me down in the Good Life café on St John's Wood High Street and told me the news that I knew was coming: my England central contract was not being renewed. It was no surprise. It was September 2017, and the sum total of international cricket I had played over the last twelve months was four ODIs and a solitary Test match. It hurt to lose my central contract and all the perks that came with it after seven years with one, but it only underlined what I already knew: I had slipped down the pecking order and needed to get myself out of another rut if I was going to become an England regular again.

Strauss was the managing director of England cricket by now, and knew the importance of clear communication from his time as captain. He wanted to tell me about my contract in person rather than on the phone or in an email, which I respected, but he said something else that sent a jolt through me. I had been anticipating the contract news when I walked into that meeting, and he was only stating the obvious when he told me that I wasn't really in England's plans as things stood; I had worked that one out for myself when I was left out of squads, and I'd only had occasional glimmers of the 2015 version of me throughout the summer for Middlesex.

What I hadn't expected was for him to tell me that the next time I played for England would be my last chance. I'd had enough opportunities to prove myself, Strauss said, and it was time for me to start delivering. If I didn't make the most of my next call-up, then that was it.

I still get on well with Strauss all these years later, and we reminisce about the great times I had playing under his captaincy whenever we bump into each other. But I've never asked him about that conversation again, and the reason he said that. Did he have some misguided sense that I was lazy, and needed a rocket up my backside? Was he punishing me for my criticism of the selectors – and, by extension, him – when I was removed from the World T20 squad eighteen months previously? Or did he genuinely mean it, and want to lay things out as plainly as possible for me so that I would realise my career was in danger of drifting away from me? I still wonder whether it was a useful thing for me to hear. It was incredibly confronting: I was only twenty-eight, after all. Yes, I had played for England for a long time, and no, I hadn't ever quite fulfilled the incredibly lofty expectations that people had placed on me when I was barely twenty-one. But I felt as though my future still involved many more international appearances, both in white-ball cricket and at Test level. Little did I know that I had already played my last game for England.

It was a brutal winter away in 2016/17, one of the longest of my career. It is tough spending the best part of six months away from home at the best of times, but even tougher when you're hardly playing. Don't get me wrong: I loved the opportunities I had to play international cricket, and wouldn't change them for anything. I had some amazing times touring overseas, exploring some incredible countries with some of my closest friends. But by the end of 2016, I was desperate to get home. We had arrived in Bangladesh at the end of September to presidential-level security after a terrorist attack there earlier in the year, and by the time we played the fifth Test of the tour to India that followed, we had been on the subcontinent for nearly three months. To make things worse, I hadn't played a single game across two months in India – we didn't even have any warm-up fixtures for a run-out between Tests – and I had flashbacks to the 2013/14 Australia tour, where I was making myself a worse bowler by grooving bad habits in the nets. I was nowhere near as bad as then, but I was trying my hardest to replicate any semblance of intensity in training and to stay on top of anything technical that may be creeping in by only bowling in the enclosed environment of the nets. Alastair Cook always used to bring a dartboard on tour with him, which took a peppering on that trip. During the final Test in Chennai, I had a day off from twelfth man duties. I went to the team room in our hotel and spent four hours throwing darts by myself; each thud of a dart landing marked another second closer to the plane home. At least I hit my first-ever 180 which, sadly, was the highlight of my entire trip.

The winter started with an ODI series in Bangladesh, which I initially saw as a great opportunity. I was a late call-up to the squad when Mark Wood went down injured, but felt confident that I had finished the season strongly with Middlesex and would be given a chance to lead the attack. It was a year since I'd last played for the white-ball side, and I saw this as my route back in. We were missing Eoin Morgan, who along with Alex Hales had decided not to tour due to the security situation; to be honest, I had underestimated how intense it would be. Whole cities were effectively shut down just so that we could travel back and forth from training sessions in an armed convoy, and there was never any question of us leaving the hotel for a bite to eat down the road. It was a total lockdown, and the first time in my career that I had experienced anything so suffocating. Jos Buttler, another close friend of mine, deputised as captain, and came to my room the night before the first ODI to deliver some bad news. Jake Ball, who had broken into the Test team that summer, was going to play ahead of me because they wanted to have a look at what he could do with the white ball; he took a five-for on debut, which meant I was on the back foot for the tour straight away. I was already staring down the barrel of three long months ahead.

I ran the drinks throughout the ODIs and for the first Test too, but was back in the side for the second, with Stuart Broad rested ahead of the India series. I tried not to put too much pressure on myself – I knew that Trevor Bayliss thought I could bowl – but I was conscious that I hadn't taken many wickets in the summer, and the second Bangladesh Test was my chance to put my hand up for selection ahead of five matches in India. The trouble was, we were playing at Mirpur in Dhaka, which must be one of the most spin-friendly pitches in world cricket: Bangladesh only picked one seamer, who bowled three overs in the match, and loaded up on spin. I was happy enough with how I bowled in the first innings under the circumstances, but the pitch was offering so much assistance for the spinners that I was barely used. I bowled eight overs in the first, three in the second, and that was that; much as I was frustrated not to get an opportunity with the reverse-swinging ball, it was never going to be a match that I dominated. Bangladesh played brilliantly, and ran through us on the third day to beat England for the first time in their Test history. It was a massive scalp for them, and I realised the extent of it when I was trapped lbw by Mehidy Hasan Miraz for the winning moment. As their players tore off in celebration, grabbing stumps as souvenirs and charging around the outfield, I stood there like a lemon, signalling for a review to umpire Kumar Dharmasena without realising that we didn't have any left. Of course, it didn't even cross my mind that this could turn out to be my final act as a Test cricketer.

The India series was a real grind. I had good memories there from the 2012 tour, but we no longer had spinners of the same calibre as Graeme Swann and Monty Panesar, and India had become a real force again, too. I was never even close to playing in any of the five Tests, and found myself chasing my tail again – just like the 2013/14 Ashes tour. I have a vivid memory of Cooky coming up to me on the dressing room balcony at the Wankhede Stadium before the fourth Test in Mumbai, and telling me he needed to chat to me about something, but neither of us followed it up. I never found out what it was. Maybe he was just worn down by the captaincy: we lost a tough series 4–0, and he stepped down soon after; you could tell by the end of the trip that his candle had completely burned out. I spent those six weeks bowling in the nets, bowling myself into worse rhythm by not playing, and becoming hyper-aware of my bowling action. I was videoing every nets session and worrying about little technical details when all I really needed was to decompress. It brought back a lot of bad memories: I was so wary of how I had felt by the end of that Australia tour that I managed to catch myself before things really spiralled, but I remember coming home from India feeling like a worse bowler than I was when I flew to Bangladesh three months previously, mentally and physically drained.

We went to the West Indies for a short tour – two warm-up games, then three ODIs – in early 2017, and I finally returned to the white-ball side. My body was causing me all sorts of grief again: I had been racking up the air miles, flying into the Caribbean after a short trip to Dubai as a replacement player in the Pakistan Super League, and my left knee swelled up really badly during our first warm-up match in St Kitts. It was so swollen that I struggled even to bend down to pick the ball up while fielding, but I was determined that my body wasn't going to cost me another opportunity. It was no surprise that my knees suffered as my career went on. I was lucky in that I hardly had any serious injuries between turning professional and the age of twenty-seven, but the flip side was that my body rarely had a break from the strains of bowling fast. The force that goes through a fast bowler's braced front leg at the point of delivery is about eight times their body weight, so you can only imagine how much stress has gone through mine over my lifetime.

I was picked ahead of Ball and Tom Curran, who had burst on to the scene for Surrey, for all three ODIs and bowled decently. I took the new ball, which I loved, especially in white-ball cricket. I dealt with the swelling in my knee, avoided making a big deal out of my injury, and took four wickets in the series as we won 3–0. As a fast bowler you rarely bowl 100 per cent fully fit. I understand that, and it's why I would so frequently play with niggles or aches; every bowler of my generation and before would do the same. Attitudes have changed in the modern era, and I'm not sure it's for the better. We will probably never see bowlers with the same resilience as Broad or Anderson – who racked up over 350 Test caps between them – again.

We had a lot of fun on that tour and I could sense the excitement around the white-ball set-up, with an exciting group of young players who were all developing together. I showed off my footballing skills in the first game, kicking the ball on to the stumps from close range to run Jason Mohammed out then wheeling away and mimicking the France forward Antoine Griezmann's 'Hotline Bling' celebration. The second game, in Antigua, featured my 100th ODI wicket, a catch off my own bowling as Kieran Powell skied one up in the air. I briefly felt like I might be back in vogue in the white-ball team after opening the bowling, but I soon came crashing back down to earth.

Strauss had introduced a 'North vs South' series as part of his master plan to reinvigorate England's white-ball cricket. The idea was that players on the fringes of international selection could play some more competitive 50-over cricket in front of the England management, and that the series would help to bridge the gap between county cricket and one-day internationals. I thought it seemed like a good idea, but it had never even occurred to me that I might be picked for it: I had to fly from the Caribbean to Dubai to play three more games at the end of a long winter, and it felt like a kick in the teeth. It wasn't all that long ago that I had been number 3 in the world rankings for ODI bowlers, and I had just taken my 100th wicket in the format for England. Now, I was having to sing for my supper to prove that I was still good enough to be in the squad, playing in games that were ultimately meaningless in front of empty stands. Don't get me wrong: I had a fun couple of weeks hanging out with my mates in Dubai, but it was a wake-up call that I was a lot further away from where I wanted to be than I had thought. I stayed in Abu Dhabi for another couple of weeks for Middlesex's pre-season tour to complete a challenging winter: I felt like I had hardly played any cricket, yet spent the best part of six months stuck in hotel rooms.

I could really have done with a break at the start of that season to freshen up mentally, but I never got it. I bowled all right in the first few County Championship games for Middlesex, without ever setting the world alight: a couple of good performances, a couple of indifferent ones. The pitches at Lord's were slow that year, and there would barely be a slip in place for the entirety of the innings. It wasn't conducive to finding the zip and bounce I felt I'd been chasing all winter. This was highlighted when we came up against Kumar Sangakkara. He scored twin hundreds against us for Surrey, and I felt totally inadequate bowling to him. I realised that other bowlers were edging past me in the pecking order, too: Toby Roland-Jones had caught the selectors' eyes after his role in our title win the previous year, Tom Curran was making good strides, and Craig Overton was attracting attention down at Somerset. Looking back, I wish I had taken a couple of weeks out of the game to reset and refresh, but I was really keen to help Middlesex push for back-to-back titles and I still felt the good days were within touching distance. The odd ball would fly through, the odd spell would make me feel like the best version of me. But they were still infrequent and it was incredibly frustrating.

As expected, I missed out on the squad for the Champions Trophy and so, with a rare gap in our schedule, I went on holiday with my then-partner for a few days at the end of May. I woke up in Mykonos feeling a bit dusty after a night out, and realised my phone was blowing up with missed calls from Angus Fraser and Eoin Morgan. Gus told me I was needed at Lord's for an ODI against South Africa: a few players had picked up niggles earlier in the series and were being rested ahead of the Champions Trophy, so Toby and I were both going to play. The problem was, the game was starting at 11 a.m. the next day. Much as I was excited to get an unexpected opportunity to play at Lord's in front of 25,000 people, I was hung-over on a Greek island; I like to feel as prepared as possible, and this was hardly the perfect lead-in. I jumped on the first flight home that I could find. I got to the ground really early the next day, conscious that it was a week or so since my last bowl and I went through all my skills extensively in order to feel best prepared. I then sat in the dressing room watching our top order collapse to 20 for 6 on a green-top. Great.

I bowled fine, without taking a wicket, and sat in the dressing room afterwards with Toby; I was chuffed for him that he had made his international debut. It was great to see him in an England shirt: he was a later developer than me, and had to earn his opportunity through sheer hard work and volume of wickets in county cricket. He was a year older than me, and the fact that the selectors were giving him a debut at twenty-nine reassured me that I still had plenty of international cricket ahead of me. I still saw myself as relatively young in terms of age, and was as hungry as ever to play for England. Just like in Bangladesh the previous winter, I never once considered that this would turn out to be the last time I played a game of cricket for England, in any format.

I was brought into the Champions Trophy squad midway through the tournament when Chris Woakes went down injured, but never felt close to playing. I was in a couple of Test squads, too, but rather than pushing for selection I knew that I was only there on standby in case someone got injured. The truth is, I didn't bowl at all well that summer. I knew that I was surviving on the fumes of the fact that Bayliss knew what I was capable of, rather than any recent form, and recognised that the guys who were jumping ahead of me in the pecking order deserved their opportunities. I was mentally fried after the comedown of my various injuries and a long winter away, but I never felt as though I could go up to anyone and say, 'Look, I need some time off here.' I think attitudes have changed enough since then that someone in the same position would be able to switch off, take themselves out of the firing line for a couple of weeks and come back refreshed, but it didn't ever feel like an option available to me. Maybe I just wasn't strong enough in conveying with conviction what I thought was best for me. But I always felt as though I'd have been laughed out of the room and told that I was being paid to play cricket, not to sit on my backside.

I thought long and hard about leaving Middlesex that summer. I had an inkling before Strauss confirmed it that my central contract was unlikely to be renewed and with my county deal also coming to an end, it was a natural time to explore my options. There was some interest from Essex, who had just been promoted to Division 1 and ended up winning the title that year, but I was leaning towards Lancashire for a long while. I thought that their pitches at Old Trafford might have suited my style of hitting the pitch hard, and then getting reverse swing towards the latter stages of an innings, and saw myself enjoying the challenge of playing for a club with such esteemed history. In hindsight, I probably should have taken the leap: it would have meant moving up to Manchester and away from my friends and family, but it would ultimately have been a good thing for my career at a time when I needed a change.

But I felt almost duty-bound to stay at Middlesex, not least because we had such a strange season. With a near-identical squad to the one that won the title, we headed into the final month of the summer under threat of relegation, and I felt responsible for how challenging we'd found the season. Early on in the season we needed two wickets to beat Essex at Lord's with the light slowly starting to fade, but we weren't allowed to use the floodlights as the MCC would only use them for major matches. We had to sit on the edge of the pitch for half a day waiting to get back on, but we never did. Our game against Hampshire was almost entirely wiped out when the covers leaked at Uxbridge, and it turned into a last-minute scramble for bonus points. It really felt like nothing went for us that year. The final month of the season was awful. We had a bizarre incident at The Oval where our match against Surrey was abandoned on the final day because someone had fired a crossbow on to the outfield. It was every bit as strange as it sounds, and it denied us the chance to get our over rate back to where it needed to be as the game meandered towards a draw. We were docked two points and ended up going down by exactly one.

I thought I had kept us up in the penultimate game at Lord's, where I took 8 for 79 on the final day to run through Lancashire and give myself confidence that I wasn't as far away from my best as I feared, but we were met by a shocker of a pitch when we headed down to face Somerset in the relegation decider. We turned up at Taunton with Ollie Rayner, our big off-spinner, ruled out through injury, and were welcomed by a pitch with rake marks on it. I still maintain that we should have picked John Emburey, my first Middlesex coach: he'd have been sixty-five by then but was still taking wickets in club cricket, and would have found a lot more joy from that pitch than any of our fast bowlers did. It was a bleak end to the season, getting out of the away dressing room as quickly as possible while Somerset celebrated staying up. Not only had I just lost my central contract, I would now be spending the start of the following summer playing in Division 2.

I didn't have long to mope around. Straight after our relegation, I was off to Amsterdam for Jos Buttler's stag do. Going on the trip felt like an act of rebellion after losing my central contract. Cricket was briefly front-page news that month after Ben Stokes's arrest following a street fight in Bristol; he was later cleared of affray. Strauss rang around begging several England players not to go. He was worried that we'd do something stupid, and must have been under pressure from above to avoid any further damage to the game's image. A few guys pulled out, but I decided I was going regardless. If my central contract isn't getting renewed, I thought, I'm not an England player any more. So who is Strauss to tell me whether or not I should go to Amsterdam for a stag do? Jos was one of my closest mates in the England team, and I wasn't going to be pushed around by someone who no longer had any authority over me. The fact that Eoin Morgan, who was the one-day captain and a good friend, also decided to come reinforced that I'd made the right call.

We had a great laugh on the first day – at least, right up until Eoin and I realised that our phones were blowing up with calls and messages. I have a clear memory of a text from Strauss: 'Do you realise you are the top story on MailOnline, in the *Sun*, and trending on Twitter for what you've been up to in Amsterdam?' I'm not sure I've ever sobered up quicker. I racked my brains but couldn't think of anything outrageous that I'd done, then opened Twitter and saw a picture of me grinning from ear to ear while holding up a humungous dildo. It had felt like harmless fun, nothing but a group of pissed-up blokes having a laugh on a stag do. Someone had decided, as a joke, to buy a sex toy that came around the city centre with us; we threw it around, playing catch with it as we walked between bars. Of course, Jos and Eoin were smart enough to steer well clear of it, but there I was, sticking out like a sore thumb at six feet eight inches and waving it around like I'd just taken five wickets with it. It was embarrassing to get caught on camera, and I knew Strauss was livid, but I couldn't help but see the funny side of it.

Barely a week later, I got an unexpected call-up to the Ashes squad for the 2017/18 series in Australia. It came from nowhere, really: I'd had a poor Championship season by the standards I set myself, with 34 wickets at 31. But Stokes had been withdrawn from the squad, and the selectors decided to replace him with a fast bowler rather than an all-rounder. My eight-for against Lancashire had given me a lot of confidence and I'd bowled with good pace again, which catapulted me back to the top of the queue. Whereas previous Ashes series had always been long-term ambitions of mine, I honestly hadn't given this one much consideration. I had slipped down the pecking order to such an extent that I had no expectations of being named in the initial squad, and my late call-up came as a nice surprise. I went down there with a degree of optimism that I'd be part of another Ashes-winning squad, and, although I was a late addition, I thought that a strong start to the tour in training and the warm-up games would give me a chance of playing in the first Test in Brisbane.

We'd always meet up the night before flying to Australia and sleep in an airport hotel, and found ourselves in a conference room near Heathrow listening to Strauss giving us a presentation. Clearly, he was worried about the temptation for us to misbehave at a time when English cricket's reputation was in disarray. He'd put together a PowerPoint telling us how much money came into the game through sponsorships, and how many companies had already threatened to pull out after the Stokes incident. He put up a slide showing all of the negative headlines that we had created, and I burst out laughing: in among a host of newspaper front pages, there I was on the screen, holding up a giant dildo. 'It's not fucking funny!' Strauss barked back at me. The irony of the fact that his Ashes-winning team in 2010/11 had far more to drink on that tour than almost any England squad since must have been lost on him.

My series was over before it had the chance to get started. I've always been dreadful with jet lag and arrived late to the first gym session of the tour in Perth after sleeping through my alarm. We went down to Richardson Park to train and started with a middle practice: I bowled around the wicket to Cook and started a little too short before my memories of Australia kicked in. I started to find my rhythm and remembered that I could afford to pitch the ball a bit fuller because of the bounce from Australian pitches. 'This could be fun,' I thought as I beat Cook's outside edge and headed off for a bat in the nets. Paul Collingwood, by then an assistant coach, was wanging balls at me with the sidearm. After a couple of forward defences, I rocked on to the back foot and turned one into the leg side towards the midwicket region, then pushed myself forward to go and pick the ball out of the side of the net.

As I went to grab it, I collapsed in a heap. I had a horrible, excruciating pain in my left knee, and knew immediately that something was badly wrong. The joint had been sore for a while as a result of the wear and tear of the last few years, but something in the twisting motion of going to fetch the ball must have triggered something. I was rolling around on the floor while everyone looked at me and thought, 'How can this bloke have done himself this much damage while bending down to pick a ball up?' I'd managed to tear the cartilage in my knee – my interior meniscus – and it was totally fucked. I flew down to Adelaide with the team to have more scans and keep getting assessed by the physios and to try a few injections into the knee to see if it would settle at all, but it became clear very quickly that it wasn't going to get better anytime soon. I was told that I needed to go home for surgery, and needed to see the best surgeon around who was based in London. The result was that for the second Ashes tour in a row, I was sent home – but this time, rather than being after ten weeks, it was after less than ten days.

I went to see Andy Williams, an incredible surgeon who has operated on many of the world's top sportspeople. He took a look inside and told me that my knee looked a bit of a mess. I had a huge lump of cartilage floating around in my knee which had lodged between the two bones when I bent down in Perth, which was the main source of my pain. I also had something called an osteochondroma on the inside of my knee, a benign tumour the size of a golf ball. I had double surgery a few days later: an England physio, Ben Langley, came with me to the surgery and took videos and photos on his phone to show me how savage the procedure was. Andy used what looked like a carpenter's chisel and a hammer to remove the osteochondroma, and more intricate tools to get rid of the cartilage. I knew that I was out for a while as soon as I saw them, and realised almost immediately that this was the result of just how much I'd bowled in my career. There were certain constraints on your workload in matches as a teenager, but as soon as I turned professional, I had just bowled and bowled, and bowled a bit more for good measure. I also knew that all of the work I'd done in early 2014 in the Lord's indoor school had taken its toll, bowling so much on such a firm surface for two months. My braced front leg was the source of my pace when I was bowling at my quickest, and I spent years putting it under severe strain. It had finally caught up with me.

I'd had injuries before, but this was my first really serious one. My hope was that in the long run, it would make me a better bowler: I held on to the idea that I would come back in 2018 after a forced period of rest feeling mentally and physically fresh. It felt surreal being completely off the international treadmill of constantly training and playing, and being at home all winter while England were touring: even if I hadn't always played, I'd been in at least one squad for almost every overseas tour since 2010. It was bad timing after my central contract expired: I'd sustained the injury on England duty, but Middlesex were now my primary employer again. As a result, I didn't have the same access to physios and aftercare that I would have done previously, and I was floating around without any real direction.

I felt chewed up and spat out by the game, so this was a chance to decompress and take a break from spending my life at cricket grounds. I took myself off to Los Angeles for a few weeks where a few friends were based and I could switch off from the game. When I was back, I remember a surreal night out with a few of my Middlesex teammates. I was with Steve Eskinazi, Tom Helm and a few others at a nightclub in Shoreditch, and we danced along while I streamed BT Sport on my phone – propped up on a table – showing one of the Tests in Australia. I had been involved in every Ashes series since my debut, but while England were trying to get Steve Smith out yet again, I was out drinking on the other side of the world. I realised then just how far away I felt from where I'd been in the previous Ashes series, bursting back into the Test team at Edgbaston and playing a huge role in our victory.

I could blame the injury to a certain extent, but I knew deep down that it ran much deeper.

I refused to admit it for a while, but the honest truth is that I was never, ever the same bowler again after that surgery. I never even threatened being in an international squad after that winter because I just wasn't the bowler I used to be. I had the odd day where the ball came out how I wanted it to, but fundamentally I was done. I didn't want to let myself think like that: clearly, if you're playing professional sport and you're admitting that you're a shadow of your old self, then you're leaving yourself in a very vulnerable position. But when I look back, it is clear and obvious to me that the knee injury I sustained that day in Perth affected every component of my bowling action.

The biggest problem was that I no longer had the ability – or the confidence – to fully brace my front leg, which then affected the pace I could bowl at. It also changed the angles of my bowling, which then affected my accuracy as my arm, inadvertently, became much lower. I had surgery on the same knee in 2018 at the end of a frustrating summer. I went back to the PSL just before that season, which Gus advised against: he thought I was rushing back from rehab to chase a quick buck. It was an amazing experience, sharing a dressing room with guys like JP Duminy, Misbah-ul-Haq and Andre Russell; I felt a really warm reception from the fans when we travelled from Dubai to Karachi for the final, given how little cricket had been played in Pakistan over the previous decade. It showed how quickly English attitudes towards franchise cricket changed – a few years later, I would have been encouraged to go – but with hindsight, Gus was probably right. My knee flared up again, and wasn't quite right at any stage that summer. I was having fluid drained from my knee before almost every game I played and I maxed out the amount of cortisone and PRP (platelet-rich plasma) I was allowed to put in my body in an attempt to get fit. I felt like I spent the whole season with needles sticking out of my knee. None of it worked. By September, I was back under the knife with Andy. The anaesthetist even said he remembered me from the previous year as if I was returning to a hotel on a post-season holiday.

It was the following year, in 2019, that Rob Key, who would later become England's managing director, came up to me ahead of a T20 Blast game down in Taunton. Keysy was working for Sky Sports, and asked innocently whether I had changed my load-up in my bowling action because he thought he had spotted a difference. I told him I hadn't, and that as far as I was concerned, I was just trying to run up and bowl in the same way that I always had. But it set off an alarm bell in my head: clearly, I no longer looked like myself when I bowled. Subconsciously, I was compensating for the fact that my front leg was no longer braced, and it had a negative knock-on effect on the rest of my action. Even if I could still hold my own occasionally in county cricket, I was never close to playing for England again.

When Strauss and I had that coffee in St John's Wood, he had passed on the details of an independent psychologist, a guy called James Bickley from Changing Minds. The fact he was independent was significant: although he had a relationship with the ECB, he wasn't part of the England dressing room, and I had full confidence that there was absolutely no chance that he'd be relaying anything to any of the coaches.

My first meeting with him was pushed back by my Ashes call-up, but I went to see him up at Arsenal's training ground in London Colney – coincidentally, right next to Watford's, where I had done my rehab in late 2015, albeit slightly bigger and a lot more modern. He gave me a tour of the facilities, then sat me down and asked me a few really simple questions about my career – specifically, about the struggles I'd had in 2013/14 on that Ashes tour. It was the first time that I had ever truly let my guard down when speaking to someone about it, and I have never cried as hard as I did in that meeting. I sat there for two hours talking about how I had got myself into that situation and the confusion and rejection that I had felt. I cried and cried and cried.

It was like he had blown a lid off the confusion and frustration that had built up over the past four years, and it all came pouring out. I had always retained that hard exterior around me, because I was always competing: there had always been a game coming up that I could use as a reason not to go and speak to someone who could help me unravel my tangle of emotions. I had never managed to admit quite how much that tour hurt me, and had always maintained that the rut I got myself into on that tour was a technical problem in my bowling action, nothing more.

My injury meant I was forced to sit back, decompress, and – with James's help – break down those feelings. It woke me up to the fact that I was far more damaged by that tour than I had ever really allowed myself to believe. It might seem unbelievable that I hadn't realised the extent of it, especially after reading my diaries from the time and my reflections on that tour. But I was so stubborn and headstrong that for years, I had shielded myself from reality.

James unlocked a vulnerability in me that has helped me become a much more rounded, better, more balanced person as a result of being able to talk about it, but it was daunting to think how much work it would take to untangle everything. I finally started to understand that I had been through a real melting point of anxiety and depression that had played out publicly, and it was the start of a long, productive relationship with James that has really helped me. In the early days of it, we were still focused on the next time that I played for England, and how I was going to make use of my last chance at international level. It was only much later that I finally let that idea go, which really helped me acknowledge the feelings that I'd had and the experiences I'd been through.

There were often moments where I struggled to let go of the sense that I had let everyone down, and would beat myself up. I found it really hard when England won the 50-over World Cup for the first time in 2019, for example. I was delighted for my friends in the team, who had achieved something incredible, but I couldn't shake the feeling that I'd had the opportunity to be a major part of that squad and had thrown it away. I watched from my sofa in West Hampstead; my flat was barely a mile away from Lord's, so I could hear the cheers just before I saw what had happened on my TV.

I felt like I'd let slip another amazing thing that I could have achieved in my career, and I blamed myself – as I always did. It evoked the same feelings that I had when I got sent home from Australia: inadequacy, rejection, failure. The difference was that by then, I could recognise those emotions in myself rather than taking them out on people I cared about: I called James the next day, and we started to unpack how I was feeling.

It was a strange time in my life. I was still only thirty, and was close to the team itself in that most of my contemporaries were still playing for England. But when it came to selection, international cricket had never felt further away. Barney Douglas, who ran England's social media channels when I was first in the team, released a brilliant documentary called *The*

*Edge* that summer, and I sat watching a preview copy of it at Radlett Cricket Club during a rain delay in a match against Glamorgan. It was all about the journey that we had been on as an England team under Strauss and Andy Flower – our steady rise and dramatic fall – and I was transported right back into that dressing room, seeing Jonathan Trott bawling his eyes out on camera and saying how much it had meant to him. As I sat watching it back, I was in floods of tears myself, wearing sunglasses inside the changing room to hide it from my teammates, but had developed coping mechanisms by then, with James's help. I didn't bowl amazingly well in that match but managed to take a five-for, including the wicket of Marnus Labuschagne, and I felt like there was someone out there looking after me. It's not like I was suddenly back to my best, but it was vindication that I could still compete at county level – even if international cricket felt miles away.

So much of my England career had revolved around the Ashes, and I wish that I could have added another chapter to this book to tell the story of how I bounced back from knee surgery to play a starring role in the 2019 series. But life doesn't always work out like that. I was never going to make that squad, so instead it marked the start of a new journey for me, as I gradually began to learn how to enjoy watching England play Australia without being in the eye of the storm myself. It was tough at first – and still can be, years later – but I actually felt really inspired that summer, watching Jofra Archer bowl with such effortless pace, particularly on his debut at Lord's. I still get excited watching people bowl so quickly in an England shirt, and Jofra's impact made me want to rediscover that part of my own game – if only my body had let me. He had a grip on all fast bowlers – past, present and future – that summer. He made our art look incredibly easy, when we all knew just how hard it really was. If I ever forgot, I only had to look down at all the scars on my left knee for a reminder.

All of a sudden, I was watching the Ashes as an England fan again, just as I had done ten years previously. But I had played roles – some small, some much bigger – in all five Ashes series in between, winning three of them, and rode the wave of some incredible highs and extreme lows. As it slowly dawned on me that my international career was over, the pain was eventually replaced with great pride at the thought that I had left a small mark on cricket's greatest series. It had certainly left one on me.

# Epilogue

I lay down on the physio bed in the home dressing room at Hove, pulled my Sussex cap over my face, and cried. I was thirty-four, playing my first competitive match in over a year after working so hard to be fit again, and could hardly move: my back had given up on me, and I knew that my career as a professional cricketer was over.

Rachel Doyle, one of Sussex's physios, was doing her best to give me treatment, and the rest of the squad and coaching staff were coming up to me to tell me that I'd be all right. But I knew straight away that I couldn't face putting myself through any more rehabilitation. Sussex's medical team – Rachel, Jon Marrale, Mat Spence and Dave McIlwaine – had invested so many hours into me, only for me to come back bowling at barely 80mph while taking up a spot that could have been filled by a young player. What was anyone gaining from it?

The same negative feelings that followed me around throughout my career came rushing back. My parents loved coming to watch me play cricket: even when I moved down to Sussex, they would drive down together for games. I felt like I had embarrassed them, and completely let them down. They'd come especially to watch me play, and were sitting with all the other friends and families at Hove, only to see their 34-year-old son hobbling off the pitch because his body wasn't up to it. I lived walking distance from the ground, and had to limp back down the street that night feeling totally flat. I spoke to James Bickley, my psychologist, the next day, and started to draft a statement for my retirement.

**14 August 2023**

Today I am retiring from all forms of cricket with immediate effect. I have been fighting a battle with my body for the last twelve months and have admitted defeat to it.

I feel incredibly lucky to have been able to play cricket as my vocation since I made my debut for Middlesex in 2005. The journey hasn't always been smooth, but I have loved it nonetheless. To have played 126 games for England, including thirty-six Tests, far surpassed what I dreamed of.

I want to thank Sussex Cricket for their support over the last twelve months especially and for welcoming me wholeheartedly into the club at the beginning of last season. It really is a great place to play cricket and I'm sorry that I wasn't able to play more of a part on the field since joining the club. I retire with some amazing memories with England, Middlesex and Sussex, shared with fantastic people. Those will live with me forever.

Thank you to all the people who have followed and supported my career, especially my parents who allowed me to chase my dream when I was a youngster. Cricket has given me a lot and I hope to give back to the game in some capacity in the future. But, for now, I'll enjoy watching on without wondering whether my body will be able to make it through another day's cricket. Thank you.

Retiring from professional sport is seriously hard. I was in my mid-thirties and still felt very young in a broader sense, but had come to the end of a journey that had started eighteen years previously, when I made my first-class debut for Middlesex. I knew I would miss the routine of heading into the ground every morning to train, seeing the same faces, and the camaraderie of the dressing room.

But the one positive of all the injuries that I had been through in the final years of my career was that I had seen it coming, and was more prepared than I might have been. My second career in the media was already up and running. I had established relationships with the BBC, TNT Sports and occasionally Sky Sports, working as a summariser on *Test Match Special* and as a studio pundit. I had an amazing partner in Amber, who had been with me throughout my injury battles towards the end of my career. Unfortunately, she never saw me play for England but she's been a rock by my side through some shit times and has always made sure there is a smile on my face, no matter how badly things were going with my injuries and the battles I was fighting inside my own head. And in truth, I felt like my race was run: I had nothing left to give as a cricketer.

It was a shame that I couldn't have ended my career at Middlesex, but my relationship with the club deteriorated towards the end of my time there for a number of reasons. I was deeply hurt by the manner of my exit at the end of 2021, and the way that it was handled. After two decades associated with Middlesex – and having quite often put my body on the line to play for them – I felt like a few people at the club were trying to get rid of me with no one willing to take responsibility for it. I think I deserved better than the tone of conversations around the prospect of a new contract, or the statement they put out announcing that I was leaving. After two decades associated with Middlesex, it felt disrespectful, and it did sting. The abrasive style of management in my last few years at the club was so far removed from what I responded to as a player, and what anyone in the modern era was likely to.

But once I had got my head around the fact it was me that was leaving Middlesex, rather than anyone making those decisions, I was incredibly excited to move down to Sussex, where I was signed as a senior player to pass on my experience to a very young bowling attack. I'd really enjoyed the chance to mentor the young fast bowlers at Middlesex – where I had relished captaining our 50-over (2018) and T20 (2020 and 2021) teams – so it felt like a really good opportunity down at Sussex, who had a young, talented squad who needed a degree of direction. I was also determined to keep playing first-class, red-ball cricket, rather than trying to throw all of my eggs in the T20 basket. Had I known how much I'd enjoy being at Sussex, I'd have loved to have had the opportunity to move there at the end of 2017, when Essex and Lancashire were interested.

Sadly, injuries meant that Sussex never saw the best of me. My final first-class match came in July 2022 – bizarrely enough *against* Middlesex at Lord's. It was a strange feeling walking into the away dressing room, but I was mainly preoccupied by my knee that week: I was staying in the Danubius Hotel, a stone's throw from Lord's, but was taking pigeon steps on the walk to the ground because of the pain I was in. I had to dose up on strong painkillers to get through the game, and found it surreal bowling to some close friends and ex-teammates, but I knew that I couldn't go on like that. I had one final knee surgery, in the hope that it would recover in time for the 2023 summer, and slowly worked my way back to full fitness over the course of that season.

I finally made my comeback in August, against Durham in the 50-over competition, and was a bundle of nerves. I hardly slept, and had the same anxiety and anticipation that I felt the night before my first Ashes Test at the Gabba, which reminded me how much I still cared about playing cricket. I beat the outside edge with my first couple of balls to Alex Lees, who had opened the batting for England the previous summer, and remembered how much fun cricket could be. Then, in my second over, my body gave up on me: I had to call the physio on after a back spasm, asking for Deep Heat and painkillers, and was so stubborn that I fought through the pain for two more overs. But I knew I was done: I hobbled off the field, clambered slowly up the stairs to the dressing room, and collapsed on the physio bed. It was over.

I'm able to reflect on my career from a distance now, and the sense of unfulfilled potential that gnawed away at me for years has been overtaken by my pride in what I did achieve. On the day that I retired, Michael Atherton wrote a lovely piece about me in *The Times* which I really appreciated, especially from the man that had presented me with my Test cap all those years ago in Chittagong. *'All told, for all the ups and downs, only twenty-four fast or fast-medium bowlers have taken more Test wickets for England,'* it finished. *'It has been a fine career.'*

I have been mindful of the ups and downs of my playing career in my work as a broadcaster. I said to myself soon after I started working in the media that I would always try to bring context and reason to my criticism: I remember how hurt I was by some of the ill-informed coverage when I was sent home from Australia, and never want to fall into the trap of being lazy in my analysis. When you are removed from the game, it's easy to feel like the players are robots, or video-game characters who should never make mistakes, but that couldn't be further from the truth. It was a fine balance to strike early in my punditry career, because you don't want your personal relationships to get in the way of giving an opinion, but I feel like I have found a way to manage it.

I'm also wary of heaping too many expectations on young players, which definitely affected me. I can understand why people got ahead of themselves: England finally had someone in their early twenties who could bowl 90mph. Why wouldn't you be excited by that? What I didn't appreciate at the time was that by reading all of the positive things people wrote about me, I was setting myself up for a fall when my form suffered. By talking people up to an unhealthy extent, you then put them on an unsustainably high pedestal. It has only become more extreme since then: cricket is a game of nuance, and a long story which develops across days, weeks and even months, and that doesn't fit easily with the modern world's desire for immediate, knee-jerk reaction. I often try to remind myself how mentally and physically challenging the game is. I played with some of England's best-ever players, but even guys like Alastair Cook, Kevin Pietersen and Jimmy Anderson went through periods in their careers where they really struggled. There's no getting around it: cricket is fucking hard.

I was first asked on to *Test Match Special* in 2019. Adam Mountford, the producer, rang me up while I was at Middlesex's end-of-season dinner to invite me on England's tour to New Zealand: he'd listened to me trying my hand as a summariser on BBC London with Kevin Hand as a young Middlesex player, and I'd clearly left a good impression on him. I jumped at the opportunity: the previous winter, I'd spent a couple of weeks doing work experience as an estate agent as I started to prepare for my post-playing career, and a month in New Zealand watching England play cricket sounded like an upgrade from Savills. There were some slow sessions during that series on some incredibly flat pitches, and I realised then that cricket commentary didn't *always* have to be about the actual cricket.

It was while working on *TMS* that I finally met my hero. I went down to Australia on the 2021/22 Ashes tour and was sitting on-air during a rain break in Hobart, chatting to Jonathan Agnew and looking out at the pitch. Suddenly, I turned around to see Glenn McGrath in the seat next to me. I was transported back to Southgate Cricket Club in 2004, where I'd been too nervous to ask him to sign my ticket; all these years later, I was live on-air talking about fast bowling with him, and finally plucked up the courage to ask him for a photo. He was friendly, gracious and clearly appreciated how much it meant to me that I had the opportunity to talk about our shared passion with him.

There have been other big changes in my life that have put the end of my playing career into perspective, and have certainly kept me on my toes. Amber and I welcomed our first child, Kora, into the world on 23 December 2024, the best Christmas present I've ever had. I never realised that I could love something or someone as much as her: becoming a dad has transformed my outlook, in that I am no longer the most important person in my own life. I didn't appreciate just how much it would affect me but it has already been the most amazing, life-changing experience, and I know we have a lot more to look forward to as a family.

I don't know exactly what lies ahead: I have loved working in the media and hope that I can be part of *TMS* for many years to come, but have also dipped my toe into administration. I became a director on the Middlesex board in early 2025, and have plans to complete my coaching qualifications, too: I relished sharing my experiences with young bowlers as my own career progressed, and would love the opportunity to pass my knowledge on to the next generation.

Retirement was a daunting step – nineteen seasons after John Emburey called me into his office to offer me my first contract, I could no longer describe myself as a cricketer when people asked me what I did for a living – but I'm at peace with it. Cricket was my whole world: I gave everything I had to it, and for all that it took out of me, it gave me plenty back along the way. Now, it is just one part of it – but one that will forever feel like home.

# Acknowledgements

My first thanks go to Matt Roller, who from our first meeting in Parsons Green to the submission of the final draft has worked so hard to bring this book to life. It's been a story I've found hard and emotional to reconnect with over the last twelve years, but I'm really thankful that we managed to put this together in tandem and feel as though we've done my career justice.

Tom Noble has thrown himself into this project and worked incredibly hard to help us turn it from an idea into reality in a tight timeframe. We are both incredibly grateful to him for the feedback and guidance that he provided, and for his patience when we found ourselves pressed for time. We would also like to thank the rest of the team at Seven Dials and Orion: Jo Roberts-Miller as project editor; Jess Hart for designing the cover; Natalie Dawkins for her work on images; and Tom Hill for his help with publicity.

My agent, Andy Hipkiss, has been a great support – both through this process, and in my new career as a pundit and broadcaster. David Luxton, along with his team at DLA, helped us both take a nascent idea and turn it into a full manuscript which we are proud of, and I know he has been a real source of calm and advice for Matt in particular from start to finish.

I have drawn primarily on my own memories throughout this text, with some help from other sources including my

# ACKNOWLEDGEMENTS

diaries, media reports and cricket websites like ESPNcricinfo and CricketArchive. I take full ownership of the accuracy of the text, and any remaining errors are my own. I am also grateful to all of those who helped jog memories during the process, including my parents, Andy Flower and Angus Fraser.

We are both grateful to those who read through drafts of chapters and provided valuable feedback, including my partner, Amber O'Shea, Susie Goldsbrough, Daniel Norcross, Tim Wigmore, Freddie Wilde and many of those names above. We would also like to thank friends, family and colleagues for their help in enabling us to pursue this project, and for their support and enthusiasm throughout the process.

Finally, I'd like to thank my countless teammates, opponents, coaches, backroom staff and everyone else involved in my cricketing journey, from age-group club cricket around Watford, right the way through to the England team. No cricketer can reach the international level without hours of sacrifice and dedication from those around them, and I will always be grateful to those that played a role – big or small – in helping me to achieve my dream of representing my country.

# Picture Credits

Page 1 2007 © Adam Davy/PA Images/Alamy; Celebrating Riki Wessels wicket, caught by Andrew Strauss © Sean Dempsey/PA Images/Alamy

Page 2 Being presented with my first cap by former captain Michael Atherton before the day's play during the First Test at the Jahur Ahmed Chowdhury Stadium © Gareth Copley/PA Images/Alamy; Celebrating the dismissal of Bangladesh's Imrul Kayes, during the fourth day of their first test cricket match in Chittagong, Bangladesh © Aijaz Rahi/Associated Press/Alamy

Page 3 Dismissing Bangladesh's Tamim Iqbal during the first nPower Test Match at Lord's and getting on the Honour's Board © Gareth Copley/PA Images/Alamy; Preparing for my Ashes debut with a nets session at the Gabba in Brisbane © Gareth Copley/PA Images/Alamy

Page 4 Dismissing Philip Hughes during the Third Ashes Test at WACA, Perth © Gareth Copley/PA Images/Alamy; With Eoin Morgan celebrating in the dressing room with the Ashes urn after winning the series 3-1 © Tom Shaw/Getty Images/POOL/PA Images/Alamy; Jonathan Trott, right, tries to drag me away as I talk to India's captain Mahendra Singh Dhoni, left, and teammate Virat Kohli, second left © Aijaz Rahi/Associated Press/Alamy

# PICTURE CREDITS

Page 5 Andrew Strauss, Tim Bresnan and I appeal to the umpire after a wicket was disallowed as the bales at the bowlers end fell off during bowling © Joe Giddens/PA Images/Alamy; Celebrating taking Ed Cowan's wicket during day one of the First Investec Ashes Test match at Trent Bridge, Nottingham © Nick Potts/PA Images/Alamy

Page 6 The side-on angle from Alice Springs in 2013/14 which revealed the 'shortness' that had crept into my action © Anthony Devlin/PA Images/Alamy; Queen Elizabeth II shakes my hand at Lord's ahead of the first day of the second test between England and Australia © Anthony Devlin/PA Images/Alamy; Celebrating taking Australia's Steve Smith's wicket during day one of the Third Investec Ashes Test at Egbaston, Birmingham © David Davies/PA Images/Alamy

Page 7 Celebrating taking the wicket of Australia's Adam Voges during day two of the Third Investec Ashes Test at Edgbaston, Birmingham © David Davies/PA Images/Alamy; Leading the walk off at the end of play after taking 5 for 45 during day two of the 3rd Investec Ashes Test match © Michael Steele/Getty Images; Fifth Test winners © Philip Brown/Pool/PA Images/Alamy

Page 8 Talking to Rob Young about my injury in Pakistan © Gareth Copley/Getty Images; Winning the County Championship with my boyhood club in 2016 was one of the happiest days of my career © Philip Brown/Popperfoto/Getty Images; I finally plucked up the courage to ask my hero Glenn McGrath for a photo during the 2021/22 Ashes tour © Steven Finn

# About the Authors

**Steven Finn** took more than 250 international wickets for England across a seven-year international career. A fast bowler, who regularly hit speeds of 90mph, Finn won three Ashes series – in 2010/11, 2013 and 2015 – and took more than 900 wickets in his eighteen years as a professional cricketer. Since his retirement in 2023, he has become a prominent pundit on the BBC's *Test Match Special* and TNT Sports.

**Matt Roller** is a journalist for ESPNcricinfo, covering international and T20 cricket around the world. He is the co-author of *White Hot: The Inside Story of England's Double World Champions* with the *Telegraph*'s Tim Wigmore, and is a regular guest on the *Wisden Cricket Weekly* podcast.

# Credits

Seven Dials would like to thank everyone at Orion who worked on the publication of *The Ashes Files*.

**Agent**
David Luxton

**Editor**
Tom Noble

**Copy-editor**
Jane Selley
Ian Greensill

**Editorial Management**
Jo Roberts-Miller
Jane Hughes
Charlie Panayiotou
Lucy Bilton
Patrice Nelson

**Contracts**
Rachel Monte
Ellie Bowker
Tabitha Gresty

**Proofreader**
Luke Brown

**Design**
Jessica Hart
Nick Shah
Deborah Francois
Helen Ewing

**Photo Shoots & Image Research**
Natalie Dawkins

**Inventory**
Jo Jacobs
Dan Stevens

**Finance**
Nick Gibson
Jasdip Nandra
Sue Baker
Tom Costello

## CREDITS

**Inventory**
Jo Jacobs
Dan Stevens

**Production**
Hannah Cox
Katie Horrocks

**Operations**
Group Sales Operations team

**Publicity**
Tom Hill

**Sales**
Dave Murphy
Victoria Laws
Sammy Luton
Group Sales teams across
Digital, Field, International
and Non-Trade

**Rights**
Rebecca Folland
Tara Hiatt
Ben Fowler
Maddie Stephens
Ruth Blakemore
Marie Henckel

# RAISING READERS
### Books Build Bright Futures

Dear Reader,

We'd love your attention for one more page to tell you about the crisis in children's reading, and what we can all do.

Studies have shown that reading for fun is the **single biggest predictor of a child's future life chances** – more than family circumstance, parents' educational background or income. It improves academic results, mental health, wealth, communication skills, ambition and happiness.[1]

The number of children reading for fun is in rapid decline. Young people have a lot of competition for their time. In 2024, 1 in 10 children and young people in the UK aged 5 to 18 did not own a single book at home.[2]

Hachette works extensively with schools, libraries and literacy charities, but here are some ways we can all raise more readers:

- Reading to children for just 10 minutes a day makes a difference
- Don't give up if children aren't regular readers – there will be books for them!
- Visit bookshops and libraries to get recommendations
- Encourage them to listen to audiobooks
- Support school libraries
- Give books as gifts

There's a lot more information about how to encourage children to read on our website: **www.RaisingReaders.co.uk**

Thank you for reading.

---

[1] National Literacy Trust, Book Ownership in 2024, November 2024
https://nlt.cdn.ngo/media/documents/Book_ownership_in_2024

[2] OECD. 2021. 21st-century readers: developing literacy skills in a digital world. Paris, France: OECD Publishing.
https://www.oecd.org/en/publications/21st-century-readers_a83d84cb-en.html